OUTPOSTS OF THE
SPIRIT

WILLIAM M. JUSTICE

OUTPOSTS OF THE
SPIRIT

HAMPTON ROADS
PUBLISHING COMPANY, INC.

Cover design by Marjoram Productions
Cover painting by Nick Gonzalez

For information write:
Hampton Roads Publishing Company, Inc.
1125 Stoney Ridge Road
Charlottesville, VA 22902

Or call: 804-296-2772
FAX: 804-296-5096
e-mail: hrpc@hrpub.com
Web site: http://www.hrpub.com

If you are unable to order this book from your local
bookseller, you may order directly from the publisher.
Quantity discounts for organizations are available.
Call 1-800-766-8009, toll-free.

Library of Congress Catalog Card Number: 99-95408

ISBN 1-57174-157-7

10 9 8 7 6 5 4 3 2 1

Printed on acid-free paper in the United States

Editor's Introduction

Why publish a book written almost twenty years ago about a rapidly evolving field that moves forward with new developments almost every month? A great deal has happened in the field of paranormal studies since the late William Justice wrote this survey. But what hasn't changed is the need for a way of looking at the field that accommodates prior beliefs, doubts, and natural skepticism. William Justice provides this masterfully, in a manner both cordial and fair, clear and incisive.

Many people have heard about the paranormal—astral projection, out-of-body experiences, life after death, talking to spirits, the Ouija board, telepathy, precognition, angel sightings, among many other phenomena—but they haven't known what to make of this baffling, seemingly uncorroborable field with its reputation of attracting frauds and eccentrics. Some may feel that the paranormal has no place in Christian belief and those with no personal experiential base may find the paranormal as inaccessible as quantum physics.

Justice offers readers from both camps an excellent bridge between everyday reality and the paranormal. He provides a safe, reliable, responsible, authoritative escorted tour through the world of paranormal phenomena, in such a way that readers are allowed to formulate their own conclusions, for or against, as each new outpost of the spirit is pointed out.

Justice, who spent his professional life as a Protestant minister, makes it clear that paranormal phenomena are detailed in various books of the Bible and attributed to key figures in biblical history, and that they are legitimate examples of "going within to communicate," of finding new ways to achieve "communion with God," as indicated in the New Testament.

Those who decide to investigate this field will find Justice an understanding and tolerant host. He admits that he has been touched by the paranormal himself, and he uses his personal meetings with luminaries in the field—he interviewed the famous "sleeping prophet," Edgar Cayce, in the 1940s—as well as correspondence from his colleagues and parishioners and his own careful reading of published accounts to put together a soundly reasoned case for granting the paranormal more credibility than many might have felt comfortable according it previously.

As an aid to the reader, we have added brief footnotes to identify researchers and key figures in the field, or explain certain terms or practices not necessarily known to everyone. Otherwise, *Outposts of the Spirit* is as vital, informative, and helpful today as it was in the early 1980s when William Justice wrote it.

Richard Leviton, Senior Editor

Outposts of the Spirit are those outpoints along the front lines to which the brave pioneers of the human race have reached in their search for truth.

Dedication

To my wife, Thelma (Dunagan) Justice,
who has been my devoted companion and
helpmate for more than fifty-five years,
and to our precious children,
Lincoln Bruce Justice
and
Ruth (Justice) Moorer
who have all encouraged me
in writing this volume.

Contents

Foreword

On August 31, 1985, my good friend and spiritual pioneer, William M. Justice crossed the border into the realm of light that he had spent so much of his life exploring.

I first met Bill Justice and his gracious wife, Thelma, on a spiritual retreat in 1970. I was impressed not only with his knowledge of the Bible, which seemed as familiar to him as his own hands, but also with his insatiable search for truth about the continuation of life after death. Over the years I was most inspired by the love, compassion, and respect he had for his fellow human beings. Remembering the words of our Lord Jesus, "By their fruits you shall know them," I recognized Bill Justice as true follower of Jesus.

After meeting so many ministers who could not comprehend the implications of my own near-death experience, it raised my own spirit to meet Bill and Thelma, who not only understood my experience but inspired me to see that it was put into a book, *Return from Tomorrow*.[1] In this way, many people could share my visit into life after death and my meeting with our Lord Jesus.

---

1   George G. Ritchie with Elizabeth Sherrill, *Return from Tomorrow* (Waco, Tex: Chosen Books, 1978).

Bill Justice has succeeded in providing in this book, through a compilation of years of personal experience and research, a lucid picture of what happens to the soul or spirit of a person when it is separated from the earthly body by death or any other cause.

He met and came to know many great searchers for truth, such as Albert Einstein, J. B. Phillips, C. S. Lewis and Edgar Cayce, as well as many other fellow seekers from all walks of life. You shall meet them also as you read this book.

God is truth and God is love. Through his search for the truth, Bill Justice helps us better understand these important facts of life. I had to go through a death experience to learn some of the great insights into the nature of God and the universe that Bill Justice shares with us in this book.

As a sincere, humble, and dedicated Christian minister, Bill Justice has done for us what we have needed for a long time.[1] At last a well-grounded man of Christ has accepted the challenge to pursue open-minded research into the unknown area of perception beyond the five physical senses. Others have had less courage. Because of their fear, they have blindly labeled everything associated with extrasensory perception (ESP) as being "of the devil."

Bill Justice has shown that the Holy Spirit of God that lives in Jesus is still in contact with us every day in ways that go beyond our five physical senses. If we actually believe what we say in the Apostles' Creed—"We believe in the communion of Saints"—then we believe that com-

---

1   During his forty-four-year ministry and beginning in 1928, Bill Justice served fourteen pastoral appointments in the Methodist Church in Texas, New Mexico, New York, and New Jersey

munication is possible now between persons in heaven and on earth.[1] I feel that Bill Justice has proved that God has always communicated with human beings through the extrasensory perception of spirit with spirit. If this is not true, how do we expect to talk with the Spirit of God in prayer or know when God is talking back to us?

All of us, in our search for God and truth, owe William M. Justice a debt of gratitude for having shared his search for truth with us.

Blessings on you, Bill, in your new adventure beyond death.

George G. Ritchie, M.D.
Author of *Return from Tomorrow* (1978)
and *Ordered to Return* (1998), originally
published as *My Life After Dying* (1991).

---

1   The Apostles' Creed is a concise statement of faith within Christian practice, often set to music; it is derived from statements believed to have been made by each of the Apostles before setting out on their missions.

Preface

There is a commonly held notion that religious claims must be taken by faith while scientific findings are based on proofs that are open to verification by all. To the contrary, it is evident that many of the things that are asserted today as positive facts by nuclear physics or astronomy are so fantastic as to be unbelievable and require as much faith to accept as any of the claims of religion, including the doctrine of the Trinity or the awesome fact of the Incarnation.

Incredible as are the mysteries of outer space that radio telescopes are bringing to light, no less so is the microcosmos. Cells, molecules, and atoms are as incredible as are constellations and galaxies. Using instruments that enlarge images with electrons instead of light rays, the atomic structure of the most minute organism can be revealed. A new area of reality, never before seen by man, has opened up, with the result that the infinitely small is found to be as mysterious as the infinitely large.

But if the outer physical universe has its bewildering aspects, still more mysterious is the inner world of the mind. Recent experiments have demonstrated that thoughts are things, that the mind can produce effects not only telepathically on other minds but also on inanimate matter as well.

Uri Geller, a young Jewish sensitive, has manifested a remarkable range of psychic powers, including the amazing capacity to bend keys or spoons or to start or stop watches by the power of his mind.[1] People gasp when a ring or key clutched tightly in their hands begins to bend and keeps on bending for minutes after Geller has passed his hand over it. Similar mental powers have been displayed by the noted artist Ingo Swann under tests conducted at the Stanford Research Institute in Menlo Park, California. During these tests, Swann has been able to change the temperature of a distant insulated object by the power of thought alone.

The often quoted remark of Shakespeare's Hamlet to his friend Horatio that there are more things in heaven and earth than are dreamt of in philosophy was occasioned by Hamlet's meeting with his father's ghost. At the time Shakespeare wrote his famous play, the reality of the supernatural was taken for granted by practically everyone; witches and goblins were accepted without much question. This was half a century before Sir Isaac Newton observed the falling apple, from which he derived his inferences concerning gravity and the laws of motion. But following Newton's epoch-making observations, the reign of immutable law was ushered in and physical science took over as man's new religion. The prevailing scientific viewpoint since Newton's day can be

---

1   Uri Geller (b. 1946 in Israel) gained considerable public attention in the 1970s for his ability to bend metal objects by either touching or looking at them, and to stop watches or make them keep time faster. These psychokinetic effects became known as the "Geller effect," which he often demonstrated in public. In 1975, Geller published *Uri Geller, My Story* (London: Robson Books, 1975) and in 1987, *The Geller Effect* (with Guy Lyon Playfair, New York: H. Holt and Co., 1987).

expressed in materialism's original dictum that the universe is made up of ether and atoms and there is no room for ghosts.

The agnostic materialism of the past two centuries has denied what George Tyrrell, the Roman Catholic theologian,[1] says distinguishes religion from ethics: "belief in another world and the endeavor to hold intercourse with it." These two basic assumptions—that there is a spiritual world and that it is possible for a person to carry on commerce with it—provide the preamble to all religions. According to orthodox science, there is no spiritual order beyond the physical world of the senses and, therefore, no commerce is possible between the seen and the unseen worlds.

But a significant reaction to this rigid skepticism concerning metaphysical realities has been taking place among reputable men of science within recent years. One example of this changed attitude on the part of orthodox physicists is that of the astronaut Edgar Mitchell, who conducted an experiment in telepathy while on the January-February 1971 Apollo 14th flight to the moon. He turned from a career in the National Aeronautics and Space Administration to set up a corporation called the Institute of Noetic Sciences for the study of human consciousness.[2]

Even more significant is the remarkable change in the public mind toward the reality of metaphysical matters

---

1   George Tyrrell, Irish Catholic theologian (1861–1909); author of *The Faith of the Millions* (1901), *Medievalism* (1908), *Christianity at the Crossroads* (1909), and *Autobiography* (1912).

2   The Institute of Noetic Sciences is still flourishing, located in Sausalito, California, where they publish newsletters and sponsor conferences and research.

during the past quarter of a century. A nationwide survey conducted by the University of Chicago's National Opinion Research Center[1] revealed that 63 million Americans—one out of three adults—say they have had a powerful supernatural experience. A total of 36 percent of those interviewed said that they had felt at some time in their lives as though they were close to a powerful force that seemed to lift them out of themselves. Some 61 percent told of having the déjà vu experience, and 34 percent reported that they had had contact with the so-called dead.

Such changes suggest that we are on the verge of a massive breakthrough into a new world of reality. New areas of human consciousness are opening up. A growing number of persons claim to have had incredible experiences of astral travel. Persons of little or no musical ability have been receiving compositions of high quality that they claim have been given them by the great classical masters of long ago, masters such as Mozart, Schubert, and Beethoven. Mysterious voices are being heard on electromagnetic tapes, with no explanation as to how or from where they originate.

My personal interest in the metaphysical began some forty years ago. At that time, there were very few books available in the field. I eagerly read all I could find in the local libraries; eventually, the list of books I had read grew to several hundred. In addition, I began a spiritual journey in which I took opportunities to seek out highly gifted persons in various parts of the world who had had supersensory experiences or who were working experi-

---

1   This report was called "Study of the Ultimate Values of the American People: A National Survey of Religious Behavior and Beliefs (Including Questions on Paranormal Experiences)," and was released in 1972.

mentally in the area of psychic research. Many of these persons were endowed with spiritual gifts of rare power and sensitivity. True, I met a few screwballs on the way, but in the main, my contacts were with highly intelligent individuals of unquestioned integrity in Europe and America who were specifically engaged in investigating paranormal phenomena or were themselves authentically endowed.

These persons generously received me into their homes or offices, and in many cases they gave me hours of their time, sharing their gifts and interest with me without stint. What they had, they gave freely. I learned much from them and am deeply grateful for the contribution they have made to my life and thought. In the chapters that follow, the reader will be introduced to a number of these interesting personalities, many of whom have since become close friends.

This book chronicles my search for evidence of the paranormal and my contact with persons who freely shared the remarkable experience of their spiritual gifts with me.

The breakthroughs taking place in psychic research have both scientific and religious significance. In sharing my journey, I hope that you, too, may be opened up to a new world of spiritual reality.

Acknowledgments

Heartfelt thanks to Mrs. Ree Sheeck, who spent countless hours in editing the manuscript for publication, and to Leo Yates, who, as a labor of love, took on the task of overseeing the publication when my health and strength failed. Also, special thanks to those who gave permission to use descriptions of their near-death and out-of-body experiences.

one

The Search Begins

It is generally assumed that all persons have some psychic ability latent in their makeup. The word psychic comes from the Greek word meaning mind or soul. The difference among persons in this respect, like that of musical talent, seems to be merely a matter of degree. While most people have a slight or modest measure of musical talent, only a few become masters of the art. In the same way, some psychic ability seems to be present in nearly all persons, but only the rare few have mediumistic powers of the highest order.

For myself, I have not been among this latter favored group. Odd and bizarre occurrences, such as supernatural voices, visions, apparitions, and other things of that sort, have left me mostly alone. For the most part, nothing has ever taken place with me personally that could not be explained in the ordinary way that one might explain any natural occurrence. There have, however, been a few significant exceptions, three of which stand out as having characteristic qualities of the mystical and supernormal about them.

The first of these experiences took place on a summer morning when, as a child of four, I played with my two sisters in a pasture near our Texas farm home. I became separated from them as I played and found myself momentarily alone in a cluster of cedars. As I stood there, a hush came over things; instantly, the vividness of life increased a hundredfold. The landscape about me appeared as a blaze of glory and I found myself surrounded by a shimmering sea of radiant light that flooded every tree and twig and blade of grass. It was as though a second sun had arisen at high noon. There was an aliveness about the encompassing light that pulsated with mystical beauty and joy. As Dante expressed it, "Methought what I beheld was a smile of the universe."

There was nothing spooky about my experience. It was the easiest, most natural thing imaginable and came as no surprise. At the time I seemed to know that this was true reality and that just behind a curtain, which a gracious spirit had drawn back for me, lay a world whose beauty is beyond description. I cannot say how long the ineffable vision lasted. I must have stood for several minutes transfixed by its wonder. The sensation was exquisite beyond words, and if the momentary thing had been extended and continued indefinitely, paradise itself could not have been better. Regretfully, I have never had another such experience, but I have often wished for it with a nostalgic wistfulness that is sometimes painful.

A second event having psychic qualities took place in my early teens. For a period of several years, I had had occasional occurrences of what the French call the déjà vu experience, an experience common to a large number of people. The term means "already seen" and is the sudden feeling of familiarity that sometimes sweeps over us of having been here before, as if at some indefinite past time, in just this place, with just these people, we were saying or doing just these things. The impressions would come to me with varying degrees of vividness and definiteness. I could never be quite sure whether they were the memory of an actual dream while sleeping or simply the product of mental images born in my waking moments. However, they always carried a certain freshness and familiarity that was electric. One such experience I had, which would appear to be a combination of déjà vu and precognition (seeing or knowing future events), was so definite and clear-cut as to stand out with special significance.

My two sisters and I were assisting a neighbor, a Mr. Davis, with his farm work in a fifty-acre field several miles from our home. None of us had ever been in that particular field before, but on our arrival in the early morning, there flashed into my consciousness the vivid certainty of having seen it on some previous occasion and of my being there under the immediate, identical circumstances. I knew it to be no actual dream, but for want of a better word, I described my impression to my sisters by saying, "I dreamed that the three of us were working today in this very field and that at lunch Mr. Davis and another man rode up on horseback and talked with us for a short time." To this, one of the girls replied dubiously, "Well, we'll see if it comes true."

Four hours later, while the three of us were finishing our lunch and resting at the end of the cotton rows, Mr. Davis and another man, a total stranger, did ride up. They remained in their saddles, chatted with us for ten minutes, and then rode away. There was no apparent reason for their coming by at that time. Nothing of importance was communicated in their conversation and the visit itself seemed trivial and without purpose. Yet with minuteness of detail and photographic clearness, the ritual that I had visualized would happen was carried out to the smallest particular.

How preposterous to have so distinct a dream about anything so insignificant! Granted that the visit itself was pointless, still it had the clear-cut imagery of an episode projected on a screen. The number of significant details and the vividness of the imagery made coincidence entirely too loose an explanation. The thing puzzled me at the time and left an impression of deep curiosity upon my mind.

My third experience of the supernatural, which took place during my high school days, had qualities of the weird and uncanny about it. I had just gone to live with my oldest brother, Tom, who at the time was principal of the public school in a West Texas community. Although Tom was twenty years my senior, there was a depth of affection between us that was more than ordinary. He was not only my teacher in mathematics and history in high school, but also a profound influence on my life in still more vital ways.

About a week after I arrived at his home, Tom was attending an evening meeting downtown and I was in my bedroom alone. Having completed my classroom preparation for the next day, and just before retiring for the night, I picked up a copy of the local paper and read a brief newspaper sketch about the distinguished British scientist Sir Oliver Lodge.[1] As I recall, there was nothing particularly striking or unusual about the write-up, it being simply a short summary, not more than two or

---

1 Sir Oliver Lodge, English physicist (1851–1940); investigated lightning, electromagnetic waves, and the wireless telegraph and attempted to reconcile science with religion; author of *Modern Views of Electricity* (1889), *Life and Matter* (1905), *Man and Universe* (1908), *The Ether of Space* (1909), *Raymond, in Life and Death* (1916), *Making of Man* (1924), *Beyond Physics* (1930), and *Advancing Science* (1931).

three paragraphs long, of his scientific background and interests. It made a slight reference to his interest in the supernatural.

The natural inference would probably be that the reading of the article produced a mental effect that caused what followed. Undoubtedly, the reading of it, brief as it was, opened up my mind to a new area of thought, but I do not recollect now that at the time I had the slightest uneasiness or mental agitation whatsoever after having read it. I was perfectly calm and had no anticipation of anything that was to come. At about ten o'clock, I turned off the light and lay down on the bed.

I had hardly pulled the covers about me when I felt a strange and intensified sense of the supernatural come over me that I find difficult to describe. An eerie and uncanny spirit force seemed to be present, overshadowing me. It was as if a heavy fog, which had weight about it, surrounded the bed and was closing in on me and getting inside of me.

The thing was as real as a magnetic current. It had life about it and seemed to have both an inner and an outer quality. I did not feel pain, but I did feel fear and a ghastly sort of creepiness. It was the equivalent of a nightmare while one is still awake. For the first time in my life, I felt that my conscious identity was in the grip of forces over which I had no control. I remember wondering if I were dying.

I called to my sister-in-law, who came at once, turned on the light, and inquired what the matter was. I had no way of telling her what I felt. There was nothing to be seen. I felt foolish, whereupon she remarked that it was probably a nightmare and returned to her room. But if it were a nightmare, then it was one that had taken place while I was as wide awake as I am while writing this. I did not go to sleep for a couple of hours, but lay awake, pondering the matter. The incident left me puzzled and set my mind working on what Wordsworth described as "a dim and undetermined sense of unknown modes of being."

Aside from these few personal experiences, my introduction to the field of the metaphysical came to me late in my academic training. In fact, up to the time I graduated from theological seminary and was appointed pastor of a Methodist church in a small West Texas town, I had never heard of psychic phenomena. Although I had taken a couple of required courses in orthodox psychology during college, I do not consciously recall ever having heard of telepathy or extrasensory perception in any of the classes I attended. Aside from the newspaper item I have previously mentioned, I was totally unaware of such things, had never read a book on the subject, or even knew that such books existed.

My awakening came in the form of a human interest story published in the March 1929 issue of the American Magazine. It was the account of an astonishing experience of a California journalist named William Dudley Pelley entitled "Seven Minutes in Eternity." It purported to be a report on the strange but genuine excursion of the author, who went to bed one night and, after going through the process of dying, was carried into some sort of spirit world where he met people whom he had known on earth. He returned from his amazing experience completely changed in his outlook. Because the article proved to be the epochal event that opened up for me a new area of thought and because it is significantly related to all that follows, I shall quote its essential part somewhat at length.

The episode took place in an alpine cabin in the Sierra Madre Mountains near Pasadena, California, where the author often went to do his writing. According to his account, in April 1928, he had laid in a stock of provisions and with Laska, a large police dog, as his only companion, he had motored up to his mountain hideaway to put the finishing touches to a novel he was writing. On the night of the eventful experience, Pelley lay reading in bed from about ten o'clock till around midnight, after which he turned off his light and fell asleep. His account continues:

"But between three and four in the morning—the time later verified—a ghastly inner shriek seemed to tear through my somnolent consciousness. In despairing horror I wailed to myself:

"'I'm dying! I'm dying.'

"What told me, I don't know. Some uncanny instinct had been unleashed in slumber to awaken and apprise me. Certainly something was happening to me—something that had never happened down all my days—a physical sensation which I can best describe as a combination of heart attack and apoplexy.

"Mind you, I say physical sensation. This was not a dream. I was fully awake, and yet I was not. I knew that something had happened either to my heart or head—or both—and that my conscious identity was at the play of forces over which I had no control. I was awake, mind you, and whereas I had been on a bed in the shadowy dark of a California bungalow when the phenomenon started, the next moment I was plunging down a mystic depth of cool, blue space, with a sinking sensation like that which attends the taking of ether as an anesthetic. Queer noises were singing in my ears. Over and over in a curiously tumbled brain the thought was preeminent:

"'So this is death?'

"I aver that in the interval between my seizure and the end of my plunge, I was sufficiently possessed of my physical senses to think: 'My dead body may lie in this lonely house for days before anyone discovers it—unless Laska breaks out and brings aid.'

"Why I should think that, I don't know—or what difference it would have made to me, being the lifeless 'remains'—but I remember thinking the thought as distinctly as any thought I ever originated consciously and put on paper in the practice of my vocation."

Next, Pelley felt himself whirling madly. Once an airplane in which he was riding over San Francisco went into a tailspin and almost fell into the Golden Gate Bridge. It was that identical feeling. Then someone reached out, caught him, and stopped him. A calm, clear, friendly voice said, close to his ear, "Take it easy, old man. Don't be alarmed. You're all right. We're here to help you."

"Someone had hold of me, I said—two persons in fact—one with a hand under the back of my neck, supporting my weight, the other with arm run under my knees. I was physically flaccid from my tumble and unable to open my eyes as yet because of the sting of queer, opal light that diffused the place into which I had come.

"When I finally managed it, I became conscious that I had been borne to a beautiful marble-slab pallet and laid nude upon it by two strong-bodied, kindly-faced young men in white uniforms not unlike those worn by interns in hospitals, who were secretly amused at my confusion and chagrin.

"'Feeling better?' the taller of the two asked considerately, as physical strength to sit up unaided came to me and I took note of my surroundings.

"'Yes,' I stammered. 'Where am I?'

"They exchanged good-humored glances.

"They never answered my question.

"They did not need to answer my question. It was superfluous. I knew what had happened. I had left my earthly body on a bungalow bed in the California mountains. I had gone through all the sensations of dying, and whether this was the Hereafter or an intermediate station, most emphatically I had reached a place and state which had never been duplicated in my experience.

"I say this because of the inexpressible ecstacy of my new state, both mental and physical.

"For I carried some sort of body into that new environment with me. I knew that I was nude. I had been capable of feeling the cool, steadying pressure of my friends' hands before my eyes opened. And now that I had reawakened without the slightest distress or harm, I was conscious of a beauty and loveliness of environment that surpasses chronicling on printed paper."

Pelley describes his surroundings as being a marble-tiled portico lighted by an unseen, opal illumination, with a clear-as-crystal Roman pool diagonally across from the bench on which he sat. He looked back to the two friends who had received him, and he realized that he knew them intimately; yet something about them kept him from instant identification. They continued to watch him with a smile in their eyes as he left the marble bench and moved toward the edge of the pool. "Bathe in it," they said. "You'll find you'll enjoy it."

"I went down the steps into the delightful water. And here is one of the strangest incidents of the whole 'adventure' . . . when I came up from the bath I was no longer conscious that I was nude. On the other hand, neither was I conscious that I had donned clothes. The bath did something to me in the way of clothing me. What, I don't know.

"But immediately I came up garbed, somehow, by the magic contact of the water, people began coming into the patio, crossing over it and going down the southern steps and off into the inexpressible turquoise. As they passed me, they cast curiously amused glances at me. And everybody nodded and spoke to me. They had a kindness, a courtesy, a friendliness, in their faces and addresses that quite overwhelmed me . . . I recall exclaiming to myself:

"'How happy everybody seems!—how jolly! Every individual here conveys something that makes me want to know him personally.' Then, with a sense of shock, it dawned upon me; 'I have known every one of these people at some time or other, personally, intimately! But they are sublimated now—physically glorified—not as I knew them in life at all.'

"They were conventionally garbed, these persons, both men and women. I recall quite plainly that the latter wore hats. I can see with perfect clarity in my mind's eye the outline of the millinery worn by a dignified elderly lady at whose deathbed I had been present in Sioux City, Iowa, in 1923. . . .

"I pledge my reputation that I talked with these people, identified many of them, called the others by their wrong names and was corrected, saw and did things that night almost a year ago that it is verboten [forbidden] for me to narrate in a magazine article, but which I recall with a minuteness of detail as graphic to me as the keys of my typewriter are now, under my fingers. . . . I found myself an existing entity in a locality where persons I had always called 'dead' were not dead at all. They were very much alive."

The author goes on to describe the termination of his journey—his exit from eternity, so to speak—which was as peculiar as its inception.

"I was wandering alone about the portico I have described, with most of my recognizable friends gone out of it for the moment, when I was caught in a swirl of bluish vapor that seemed to roll in from nowhere in particular. Instead of plunging prone I was lifted or levitated. Up, up, up I seemed to tumble, feet first, despite the ludicrousness of the description. A long, swift, swirling journey of this. And then something clicked—something in my body. The best analogy is the sound my repeating deer rifle makes when I work the ejector mechanism—a flat, metallic, automatic sensation.

"Next, I was sitting up in bed in my physical body again, as wide awake as I am at this moment, staring at the patch of window where the moon was going down, with a reflex of physical exhaustion through my chest, diaphragm, and abdomen that lasted several moments. . . .

"'That wasn't a dream!' I cried aloud. And my voice awoke Laska, who straightened to her haunches.

"There was no more slumber for me that night. I lay back finally with the whole experience fresh in my senses but with an awful lamentation in my heart that I was forced to come back at all. . . . Somehow or other, in sleep that night, I unhooked something in the strange mechanism that is Spirit in Matter, and for from seven to ten minutes my own conscious identity that is Bill Pelley, writing-man, slipped over to the Other Side."

The article fascinated me, but it left me wondering whether the author was telling it straight or not. The thing sounded very much as if the magazine were running short of copy and needed a sensational story to increase its circulation. Yet after my own experience at my brother's home, I could not dismiss it lightly. The article proved to be for me the breaking open of a new thought-world. Eventually, I came to know that the phenomenon, now called astral projection, or out-of-body experience, has been happening to a limited number of people throughout the centuries; a notable example is no less a person than Saint Paul himself, who mentions having had an out-of-body experience in which he was "caught up into the third heaven . . . and heard words so secret that human lips may not repeat them" (2 Cor. 12:2–4).

From this point on, I began to search for other materials in the field of parapsychology. It turned out that the high school and small town libraries in the community where we were living had practically nothing on the subject. Significantly, the first book I bought and read was William James's *The Varieties of Religious Experience.*[1] This great classic of psychology by the distinguished Harvard professor has been for me an enriching source of material ever since I first read it. I found two other books, dealing with supersensuous experiences of well-known people, interesting and valuable. The first was *The Journal of George Fox*, the story of the spiritual father of the Quakers.[2] The second was the life story of Sadhu Sundar Singh, probably the most outstanding product of the Christian missionary enterprise in India. Called *The Sadhu*, it was written by Canon B. H. Streeter of England and A. J. Appasamy.[3] The book reads like a modern version of the Book of Acts.

As I began to read further, I was surprised by the amount of careful experimental work that had been done and the extensive quantity of written material in the field of psychical research. Transcendental things have been taking place since the dawn of recorded history, but it is only in modern times that men have undertaken a serious study of them.

---

1   William James, *The Varieties of Religious Experience* (Garden City, N.Y.: Image Books, 1978).
2   George Fox, *The Journal of George Fox* (Cambridge, U.K.: The University Press, 1911).
3   Burnett Hillman Streeter and Aiyadurai Jesudusen Appasamy, *The Sadhu: A Study of Mysticism and Practical Religion* (London: Macmillan and Co., Ltd., 1921).

The first serious attempt of this sort began in England in 1882 with the formation of the British Society for Psychical Research by a small group of Cambridge scholars, including Professor Henry Sidgwick, then the most influential man at Cambridge University; Dr. Edmund Gurney; and the author and poet Frederich W. H. Myers. They were later joined in their quest by a number of other prominent individuals, including the noted physicist Sir William Barrett, Professor J. J. Thomson, the eminent biologist Alfred Russell Wallace, Sir Oliver Lodge, and William E. Gladstone, the prime minister of Great Britain.

Two years after the formation of the British Society for Psychical Research, a similar group was organized in America. Its early supporters included Professor William James, the group's first president and probably America's most honored philosopher, and Dr. James Hyslop, who resigned his chair in philosophy at Columbia University to become the full-time secretary. These men set about to study and evaluate cases of psychic happenings, with the major purpose of proving scientifically that human personality survives bodily death. The work of these societies now covers almost a century of research and investigation and constitutes a mine of carefully documented evidence of high significance.

It was only a short time after my psychic search had its beginning that we received a telegram telling us of my brother's tragic death. Several years previously Tom had given up his teaching career to enter the Christian ministry. At the time of his accident, he was pastor of a Methodist church in Arkansas. Since my high school days, he and I had maintained a close relationship with each other through personal visits and frequent correspondence. My mother, a gentle, angelic being who lived with my wife and me until her death a few years later, made the long two-day journey by train with me to attend his funeral.

On our arrival, we learned that Tom had accidentally been killed by touching a faulty electric cord attached to the washing machine while helping his wife with the washing. It would be difficult to describe how great was the loss I felt at his death. Tom was a man with exalted purpose, a kindly spirit, a contagious humor, and a discriminating sense of values. I regard him as one of the most high-minded and noble men I have ever known, and my debt to him is as great as one man can owe to another. His death gave me new incentive to my quest for empirical assurance of the life beyond.

Tom himself had a mystical bent and had known his high moments of rapture and spiritual insight, some of which had unmistakable psychic qualities about them. A few years before his death, he wrote me of one such event—a penetrating and soul-shaking experience on the order of Isaiah's vision in the temple (Isa:6). The experience occurred one day in his study while he was preparing his next Sunday's sermon. According to William James, one of the rudiments of mystical experience is the deepened sense of a word or formula that occasionally sweeps over a person and makes him exclaim, "I have heard that all my life, but I never realized its full meaning until now." It was thus in Tom's case.

The formula that triggered his experience had to do with the nature of joy. In the exalted moments of his inspiration, the insight came to him with overwhelming force that wherever the word glory occurs in the Scriptures in connection with the being of God, it may be translated as the word joy. Thus, for example, when the psalmist asserts that, "The heavens declare the glory of God," this and other similar passages may be transliterated into, "The heavens declare the joy of God." The basic truth that came to him at the moment, as he described it, was the complete and unshakable conviction that the universe is radiantly alive and animated by a living joy, a joy in which God most assuredly participates. The effect of this inspiration on him, he said, was almost more than he could stand up to, and for days he felt that he was walking on air.

My brother's glimpse into the nature of ultimate reality, the transcendent surge of joy that temporarily possessed him, was essentially of the same nature as that of Pere Hyacinthe, who was ordained a priest of the Roman Catholic Church in 1851.[1]

His death created considerable comment because of its unusual nature. Father Hyacinthe, a man of great spiritual depth and charm, died in his eighty-sixth year and was weak and feeble at the end. The night he died, not wanting to cause trouble to anyone, he said no one need pass the night near him. In spite of his objection, his daughter-in-law, Laura, who was nursing him, remained awake outside his chamber, the door of which was left slightly open.

About two o'clock in the morning she heard his voice. It was a triumphant cry. The words, "He is there!" rang out from the old priest like the blast of a trumpet. Laura sprang to him. The priest was radiant. He seized her hands. "I am overflowing with joy. You understand me, my dear girl?" No longer was he the old man of eighty-six whom she had left feeble and far gone in his

---

1   Pere Hyacinthe, born Charles Loyson (1827–1912); excommunicated for heterodoxy (1867); pastor of a liberal Catholic Church in Geneva (1873–74); founder of Gallican Catholic church in Paris (1879); author of *De la Réforme Catholique* (1872–73) and *Mon Testament, Ma Protestation* (1893).

final weakness. He seemed to have seen someone. Who was it? Why did it produce such a tremendous effect on him? What caused the joy, which did not leave him until the end? We have no way of knowing, but undoubtedly, he must have had some overwhelming vision as he was dying, such as would be called a "psychic" experience.

Significantly, many of the most exalted spirits of the race, in their inspired moments, have had the identical insight of my brother and Pere Hyacinthe—that the underlying nature of the universe is that of joy. Especially is this true of the poets and saints. Dante, in his high vision, describes Paradise as animated by "light intellectual full of love, love of the true good full of joy, joy transcending all sweetness." Dr. Samuel Johnson says of such experiences, "All those who even for a moment have glimpsed this ineffable world have longed all their waking days to recapture the experience." And C. S. Lewis, in his spiritual autobiography, *Surprised by Joy*, relates how he spent many years of his life seeking authentic joy until he was at last stabbed awake by the joy that had all the time been seeking him.[1]

A few years after Tom's death, a number of brief personal statements from eight or ten prominent American churchmen appeared in the Easter issue of the *Christian Advocate*. Published under the general heading of "Why I Believe in Immortality," one of these statements was by Dr. Sherwood Eddy (1871–1963), the author, lecturer, and internationally known Christian leader.

His testimony stood out as quite distinctive from the others. Among a number of reasons he gave for his belief

---

1   C. S. Lewis, *Surprised by Joy* (New York: Harcourt, Bruce, 1956).

in personal immortality, he said, "For the last three years, I have had firsthand testimony from scientific, psychic evidence of the survival of individual personality. Once this was a matter of faith; now it is faith plus knowledge." This statement caught my attention at once. I wanted to have more information on the subject. I wrote to the editor of the *Christian Advocate*, suggesting that he ask Dr. Eddy to elaborate on the subject and tell us just what he meant in a future article. My card was forwarded to Dr. Eddy, who in a few days replied as follows:

"Your card to Dr. Smith of the *Christian Advocate* was forwarded to me. It would take a long letter of many pages, indeed it would take a book to state the nature of the psychic evidence I have received. I can only say that over the space of three years I have had abundant, satisfying, convincing evidence of the survival of the seven members of my family who are now in the unobstructed universe. By the way, I would advise you to read that book by Stewart Edward White, *The Unobstructed Universe*,[1] or the reprint of it which is coming out every week for the last four weeks in *Liberty Magazine*. It is a thoroughly scientific and philosophical statement of the survival of personality."

Following Dr. Eddy's suggestion, I lost no time in buying a copy of *The Unobstructed Universe* and reading it. It proved to be a fascinating book that had elicited high praise from certain well-known persons such as the writer Booth Tarkington, who described it as "the most important book ever written on the most important of all subjects," and Daniel Poling, editor of the *Christian Herald*, who said, "More than anything I have read, outside of the

---

1   Stewart Edward White, *The Unobstructed Universe* (New York: E. P. Dutton, 1940).

Holy Scriptures, the book has given me strength and comfort for living."

Before the publication of *The Unobstructed Universe*, White had published two books of similar import and excellence—*The Betty Book* and *Across the Unknown*.[1] The three, taken together as a unit, represent the sum of White's experimental work with his spiritually sensitive wife, Betty, from its beginning until her death twenty years later. For the scientifically–oriented mind, the trilogy comprises three of the most significant and important books yet written on the nature of life after death. It's interesting that a number of modern theoretical physicists cautiously admit that they have derived important clues from these books for their work in nuclear experimentation.

It will be observed that up to this point in the story I had done a considerable amount of reading in the field of psychic phenomena but had had no actual contact with persons who claimed to have had firsthand experience of such things. All the evidence I had obtained was written by people whom I had never met. I had developed a keen desire to meet a few people who were themselves psychically endowed or were knowledgeable in the field of the paranormal.

About this time there appeared in print a book called *There Is a River* by Thomas Sugrue. Eventually a bestseller, it was the life story of Edgar Cayce (pronounced "Casey") of Virginia Beach, Virginia, who was at the time of publication, an almost unknown clairvoyant healer.[2] In a state of trance, he gave medical advice or "readings"

---

1   Stewart Edward White, *The Betty Book* (New York, E.P. Dutton Co., Inc., 1937); Stewart Edward White, *Across the Unknown* (New York: E. P. Dutton and Co., Inc., 1939).

2   Edgar Cayce (1877–1945), American mystic and clairvoyant healer.

that reportedly had benefited hundreds of ill persons all over the world. He had practiced medical diagnosis by clairvoyance for a number of years and had the striking power to diagnose difficult diseases while in an unconscious state, although, when conscious, he himself had only a rudimentary knowledge of medical science. The book read like a story from the Arabian Nights, and yet it presumed to be the biography of a living man who had been the means of helping hundreds of people by means of his extraordinary powers.

I became acquainted with the book through a review written by Margueritte Harmon Bro in the *Christian Century*. I had read several of her articles in various religious journals. The writer related how she had been given Cayce's book to review and was so impressed by its inherent sincerity and genuineness that she could not dismiss it as simply another book. Yet it was so bizarre that she could not lend her name to it in a review without further investigation. She did the only thing left for her to do—she caught the train to Virginia Beach and visited the Cayces for three days in their home as a guest. She came away more impressed than ever.

On reading *There Is a River* for myself, I was impressed in much the same way. From the account, it seemed that Cayce had possessed psychic powers from his childhood. In his youth, they had often been a source of embarrassment to him. He wondered if he was peculiar and puzzled over the visions and voices that came to him. A meeting with Dwight L. Moody, the noted evangelist, seemed to be the turning point of his life.[1] In the course of a conversation, the young man asked Mr. Moody if he had ever

---

1   Dwight L. Moody (1937–99), American evangelist; coauthor of *Sacred Songs and Solos* (1873) and *Gospel Hymns* (1875).

heard voices from God speaking to him, whereupon the great preacher told Cayce the curious incident that had led him on his first preaching tour of England.

According to the story, it came through a dream the evangelist had while holding a meeting in Cleveland, Ohio. In this dream, a voice directed him to close the meeting and go to London. His friends were astonished at his decision and advised him against it. Nevertheless, he later found himself roaming the streets of a poor district of London and then standing in front of a shabby tenement house to listen while a child sang "Sweet Hour of Prayer." He felt strongly impelled to enter the house, where he met a little lame girl, who exclaimed on his entering, "Oh, Mr. Moody, it is you. I read about you in one of our papers and I have been praying ever since for you to come to London." He knelt and prayed with the little girl in the first service of what proved to be the beginning of a great ministry extending throughout the British Isles.

The story, and the meeting with Mr. Moody, proved of untold value to young Cayce in causing him to believe in himself and his mission. By accident, he later discovered his ability to diagnose people's physical troubles and to prescribe remedies, abilities that on numerous occasions proved very helpful to them. The odd thing was that Cayce not only did not know medicine but often the medical words he used in diagnosing his patient's ills, while he himself was asleep, were not in his vocabulary. At first, Cayce found it hard to believe that he possessed the power to treat people in this way. Frequently, his prescription agreed with that which the doctor, to whom he sent his patients after the reading, would have suggested. At other times, they radically differed with anything the physicians might have recommended.

Sometimes Cayce's readings called for ingredients rarely used or completely unknown. Once they called for

"Oil of Smoke," something no one had heard of and that was not listed in the pharmaceutical catalogues. A second reading was taken to inquire where it could be found. The name of a drugstore in Louisville, Kentucky, was given. On wiring the manager to send the preparation, they were informed that he did not have it and had never heard of such a thing.

A third reading was taken and this time the instructions stated that the product would be found on a certain shelf in the back of the drugstore behind another preparation, which was named. The manager of the Louisville store did as instructed and discovered the bottle containing the preparation, which had been put up by a company long since gone out of business. Needless to say, after reading this story, I had a strong desire to meet the man described by the author.

The opportunity came shortly thereafter when, by appointment of our presiding bishop, we were transferred from our pastorate in Texas to a church in New Jersey. Since I would be passing through Virginia on my journey, I wrote to Mr. Cayce, asking him for the privilege of an appointment, which he generously gave me. As a result, I stopped at Virginia Beach en route to New York and spent the better part of two days with him and his associates in his home.

two

I Meet Edgar Cayce

At the time of my meeting with Edgar Cayce, relatively few persons had heard of him. Since his death in 1945, however, a movement akin to a cult has developed about him and some of his views, and he has a host of admirers. Proof of this may be seen in the enthusiasm of many young people I meet from time to time, who, on learning that I once met Cayce personally, want to "shake the hand that shook the hand." The promotional work his son, Hugh Lynn, has carried on at Virginia Beach through the organization known as the Association for Research and Enlightenment, has made Cayce's name familiar to a wide public.

The proliferation of published material relating to Edgar Cayce in recent years has made it increasingly difficult to write anything particularly new or original about him, and what I shall relate may be "old stuff" for some. However, despite all the publicity, there are still many people who are unacquainted with Cayce. For them, my description can afford an introduction to a very interesting and unusual man. Even for those who have met him in person or through the printed page, I offer here an impression of the man as seen by a psychological neophyte meeting him for the first time.

As I caught the train for my journey East, it would be hard to exaggerate the interest with which I looked forward to my visit with this unique man. My family and a small group of close friends who had read *There Is a River* shared my interest. On leaving Texas, I had promised them I would take copious notes and mail them back for everyone to read. A copy of these notes is before me as I write this chapter:

"This morning I arrived in Norfolk about eleven o'clock and secured a room at the Virginia Hotel near the railway station. I rode the bus some twenty miles to Virginia Beach and got there about three o'clock in the afternoon. I inquired at the information desk for Mr. Cayce's residence and was readily directed by a lady to a modest frame building some four or five blocks away. Cayce was in his office on my arrival and we spent thirty minutes visiting together there.

"My first impression of the man was very much as the book had described him—a humble, approachable, kindly disposed person who seemed to be as much mystified by his exceptional powers as the outsider. Since he gives two readings a day, it was necessary for him to excuse himself at 3:30 for the afternoon reading. I did not attend the session, due to the fact that the individual for whom the reading was intended was present in person and preferred that it be kept private. However, they have invited me to sit in on both of tomorrow's readings.

"While the session was being held in the rear office, I took the opportunity to examine the shelves containing Cayce's files. I found there were stenographic reports of more than 14,000 readings and also hundreds of complete case reports containing affidavits by the patients and reports by some physicians, covering a period of more than twenty years. Questionnaires have been sent to doctors who have handled Cayce's patients, asking them to give an estimate of his diagnoses, treatments, and results of his work.

"A prominent doctor in New York, who had handled some 300 of Cayce's patients, said that while the results were far from being 100 percent correct, he did rate the diagnoses as averaging 20 percent better than those of the medical experts and specialists who sent their patients to him. I understand that Cayce gives two kinds of readings—a 'health reading' in which he diagnoses the patient's physical condition, and a 'life reading' in which he offers guidance to an individual for his spiritual development.

"I was surprised to find on my arrival that Mrs. Margueritte Harmon Bro had come from Chicago and was there for another visit. Also present was Eugene Exman, literary editor of *Harper's Magazine*, who was taking notes and gathering materials for a book. On meeting Mrs. Bro, I asked her how she became interested in all this. With her characteristic vivaciousness she replied, 'Because the thing is so cockeyed!'

"Up to the present time, the public generally has not been aware of the Cayces, but in the recent September issue of *Coronet*, Mrs. Bro wrote an article about them that produced an avalanche of mail. Letters have been pouring in at the rate of seven hundred a day. The Cayces were taken by complete surprise and were unprepared for such a response. The tiny office force was swamped. They did the best they could to hastily improvise some mimeographed forms to be sent out in reply to the inquiries.

"In fact, friends who have learned of their need have volunteered assistance and are helping with the clerical work. During one of our conversations, Cayce showed me some of the stacks of mail they have received and remarked, 'I have had hardships and adversities all my life and I have stood up to them. I do not know how I shall stand up under prosperity, but I pray that I may.'

"Later in the day. Since my arrival here, I have had a couple of visits with Cayce in which we discussed a great many interesting matters, ranging from psychic things to the meaning of certain passages of Scripture. The unassuming simplicity and the kindly helpfulness of the man is very evident. His personality corresponds closely with the description the book gives—a devout Christian who regularly teaches a Sunday school class in his local church and conducts a Bible class one night each week. He reads very few books, none of them, so far as I can discover, in the metaphysical field. In fact, someone shipped him 200 pounds of books the other day, which he partly unpacked in my presence. The office staff joked about how he would place them on the shelves for someone else to read, but he would never read them himself.

"It is easy to see that a big part of Cayce's education has been derived from the Bible. Someone has said that he has made it a practice to read it through at least once a year for each year of his life. I did not go into the matter of his interpretation of the Bible. His exegesis, particularly of the Old Testament, might be rather inadequate and disappointing for the academically trained. It would probably be based more upon intuitive truth than upon historical research or critical analysis.

"Perhaps the thing that struck me most was that Cayce did not seem to have an axe to grind and was not trying to convince you of his viewpoint; rather one feels that he has arrived at his present position slowly, prayerfully, and almost against his will. Cayce is not able to explain how the giraffe got there, he simply knows it is there. He said that one surprising thing to him was that missionaries who have spent a number of years on the foreign fields in a heathen environment did not seem to have any difficulty in being kindly disposed to his work and teaching.

"In the course of our conversation, I asked him if he still had difficulty in believing his own readings, which he had had in the early years of his life. He said he had two sons and that he was grateful he had lived during the years in such a way so that he was still their hero—that both of these boys, one of whom is in the military service in England, would not make a major decision without first consulting his reading on the matter.

"While he was talking, I recalled the incident in *There Is a River* about Hugh Lynn Cayce, the son now in England. When the boy was small, he burnt his eyes so severely in a flash powder explosion that the doctors gave up hope of the child ever regaining his sight. Up to that time Cayce, although having given readings when pressed by those who came to him in desperate need, had never given a reading for any member of his own family. At the end of the week, the doctors agreed that an eye would have to be removed if the child's life were to be saved. When told this, the youngster protested to the doctors, 'If you had a little boy, you wouldn't take his eye out, would you? When my daddy goes to sleep, he is the best doctor in the world. Please, Daddy, will you go to sleep and see if you can help me?'

"Realizing that there was no other alternative, Cayce did so. The reading revealed that in addition to the solution used by the doctors, there should be added tannic acid. The doctors protested that tannic acid of the strength Cayce suggested was altogether too strong for use in the child's eyes. However, since they were sure that the sight was lost anyway, they agreed to the formula and used it. The result was that the boy not only regained his sight but, judging by his acceptance by the military, has relatively unimpaired vision as well.

"When Cayce insisted that he did not have any power that is not held in common by everyone, I asked him how he explained the fact that these powers manifested themselves through him in a way that they did not seem to do in others. He admitted frankly that he did not know, but he rather jokingly suggested that it might be because of a blow on the head as a child, or it might be his ancestors, or some other physical or spiritual cause. His sincerity, humility, and obvious desire to do good are the outstanding impressions one gets from talking with the man.

"I have just finished an extended visit with Mrs. Bro. She is a charming, intelligent woman who not only holds Cayce's psychic abilities in high regard but also has become much impressed by his readings that suggest the possibility of reincarnation (which means to take on another body with the cessation of the current one at death). She and her husband served for a number of years as missionaries in China and her oldest son, just out of the seminary, is now serving a church out of Chicago. She let me read the stenographic record of her own life reading that was given her some months back. Since that time, she has had two additional readings. The reincarnation idea came out in all three of them, as it does in practically every life reading that Cayce gives.

"An interesting thing the readings revealed was that Mrs. Bro, in one of her past selves, was the 'other Mary' spoken of in the gospels who, it turned out, was said to be the bride in the marriage of Cana of Galilee and also the 'elect lady' to whom the epistle of Second John was addressed. Mrs. Bro said that her readings were checked with one given for Sugrue and that the information derived from the readings fit beautifully together. My skepticism concerning the actuality of reincarnation being what it is, I could not refrain from jokingly suggesting to her that she appeared to be a woman of such quality and importance that anyone of my humble origin and make-up almost found himself completely out of keeping in her presence.

"There were several indications of what Cayce had meant to a number of people. For example, when a lady from Richmond whom he had previously helped heard of the flood of mail, she immediately caught the train and came down to be of assistance. In fact, a noticeable thing about the office help was that they seemed sincerely to believe in Cayce through the help he had given them. I chatted with a Mrs. Mae Verhoeven who lived at Virginia Beach and who had done a considerable bit of stenographic work in compiling materials. She was an interesting and capable woman with whom I visited for more than an hour. I asked her questions about her contact with Cayce over the past three or four years. She told me that he had been the means of changing her life, both physically and spiritually, and bringing her back to a renewed interest in the church.

"She had a good sense of humor and laughed with me as I joked with her about her belief in reincarnation. She seemingly had complete faith in the correctness of Cayce's readings along this line. She told me her readings indicated that in one of her past selves, she was one of Louis XIV's wives. I told her it was a shame that she, and others associated with Cayce, always picked out the most prominent names for themselves from those who had lived during the past and left the rest of us very few good names to choose from. I told her I really thought it a form of spiritual snobbery. She laughed, but I had the impression that she goes about considering herself Mrs. Louis XIV.

"In the evening, the two of us had dinner together in a downtown restaurant, accompanied by Cayce's secretary, Miss Gladys Davis, who has taken down in shorthand all of his readings for the past twenty years. During the meal, I asked them both a lot of questions and gleaned from them a number of curious facts on the subject of past readings. It turned out that Miss Davis herself had had numerous life readings that indicated that in one of her past lives she was Mrs. Verhoeven's daughter by Louis XIV. It was an interesting and amusing session. I told them that I was going to write home and relate how I had had dinner with Mrs. Louis XIV and her daughter. In fact, I assured them that the public in general would never realize what an aristocratic society it was at that particular table. As I rode the bus back to Norfolk following our meal, I found myself engrossed by the many new and novel ideas to which I had been exposed during the day. What a day it has been! Facts are indeed sometimes stranger than fiction.

"Next morning, due to an unexpected interruption before leaving my hotel, I was delayed in reaching Virginia Beach. When I got there, the ten o'clock reading, which I had hoped to make, was already in progress. Immediately following it, however, I had an undisturbed visit of an hour and a half with Cayce in his office. Since his early childhood, he has experienced the phenomenon of clairvoyance, the occasional ability to see people who may not be visible to others. Some of the things he told me were so incredible as to place a heavy strain upon one's confidence either in the sanity or truthfulness of the man; yet his quiet simplicity and sincerity made it hard to dismiss what he said as mere talk.

"One of the extraordinary stories he told had to do with his mother and her appearance to him after her death. A few days before her transition, Cayce's sister wired him that his mother was ill and asked him to give her a reading. Following the reading, he woke up and found his wife and children in tears. They told him that the reading indicated his mother would only live until the following Monday and that if he wanted to see her alive, he must go to her at once. Cayce took the train and when he arrived, his mother greeted him at the door, much improved. This made him feel that the reading must have been misleading; but, as it soon developed, she took to her bed again and died the following Monday.

"Cayce told me the sequel to this story that took place in 1938, a number of years after his mother's death, while he and a close friend were on a camping trip in the Southwest. At that period of his life, he had suffered a number of setbacks, both financial and otherwise, in his work. The future seemed dark and uncertain and he was greatly depressed. One evening, while his friend was asleep on the ground nearby and Cayce was sitting by the campfire looking towards the sunset, his mother appeared to him. She spoke words of encouragement and reassurance, telling him that things were going to work out well with him and not to be depressed. After visiting with him for some minutes, she left a physical token in his hand and then walked into the sunset and disappeared.

"As he finished relating the incident, Cayce opened a drawer in a cabinet near his desk, took out a small box, and said, 'You may not wish me to show you this and you may not believe what I am going to tell you, but this is the token that mother left in my hand the evening she came to me.' With this, he opened the little box and took out a silver dollar and handed it to me. The coin, which I examined, was unquestionably a silver dollar that would have passed as coin of the realm in any market, carrying the woman's head and bearing a specific date that regretfully I failed to record.

"I asked him what was the nature of such apparitions as that of his mother when she appeared to him. He said that they were tangible enough to be seen but that one could recognize that they were not composed of ordinary material substance. One thing he kept emphasizing was that while such appearances had objective existence, the value of them was largely dependent upon the spiritual help they brought to the individual at the time and were more or less conditioned by the need of the person receiving them. I was impressed by his pragmatic emphasis upon the spiritual side of things—that objective appearances may have very little significance in themselves but that it is one's inner attitude or frame of mind that is of primary importance.

"I asked Cayce if he had made any serious mistakes in the use of his clairvoyant talents. He told me that when he was inexperienced, he did not realize there was possible grave danger in his psychic gifts if they were wrongly used or commercialized. As a young man in Cincinnati, he had foolishly consented to attempt to read the races for a certain man. The first day, under Cayce's guidance, the man bet $50 on the first race and then staked all his winnings on each successive race. He made $1,800 on five races that day, and on the second day he staked his entire previous winnings and made some $15,000. The third day, on a 20-to-1 shot, he won some $200,000. Following this, the man lost his head, plunged into drink, and shortly after landed in an insane asylum.

"Cayce also referred to his experience, which Sugrue related in his book, in attempting to locate oil well sites for a drilling company, an effort that ended disastrously. He said that these experiences had taught him a painful lesson, and although he had been asked repeatedly to read the stock or grain market, he always refused. 'I have learned,' he said, 'the workings of a great law: that if you use your gifts for selfish purposes, they will prove disastrous, but if you use them to help or bless, you can use them unafraid.'

"The second reading of the day, to which I had been looking forward so eagerly, took place in the afternoon. There were five of us present in Cayce's office: Cayce himself; Mrs. Cayce, who is a slight, unpretentious woman; Miss Davis, his secretary with pencil and shorthand pad to record the reading; Mrs. Bro; and myself. The man whose life reading was to be given lived in Philadelphia and was not present. He had simply written a letter giving his name and birthplace, date of birth, names of parents, and a few elementary facts about himself that were read to Cayce by his wife after he was asleep.

"When we got into the office, Cayce took off his coat and tie and lay down upon a couch, pulling a small spread up over the lower part of his body. Mrs. Cayce sat at the head of the couch by her husband, Miss Davis next to her. Mrs. Bro took a seat a little more distant, while I got in the best possible position to get a good view of his face and the expression of Cayce's eyes. He jokingly remarked to me as he lay down that now I would get to watch what some people would call the work of the devil.

"I was careful to observe the general attitude of his wife and secretary while this was going on. In fact, I studied their faces as much as I studied his in this connection. It was plainly something they were used to doing and yet they did it with a genuine seriousness, as though they were about important business, and with something of reverence about it all.

"After lying down flat upon his back, Cayce partly closed his eyes and was in the same position in which one would be while simply resting. I cautiously took out my watch to see the time—it was twenty-one minutes to four.

After what seemed to be a slight effort on his part, his eyes began to flicker and grow sluggish, his breathing became deeper, and he appeared to be in a condition of sleep, except that his eyes did not seem to be closed in quite the same way as in normal sleep. I again checked the time with my watch and found that it had taken about three minutes for him to fall asleep.

"At this point, Mrs. Cayce read a short formula that I understand they use each time, something to this effect: now the body is before you; you will give its diagnosis clearly, distinctly, and at a normal rate of speech. Afterwards, there will be no harmful effect to the one giving the reading, but he will wake up at the proper suggestion. Following this, Mrs. Cayce read aloud the few facts given in the Philadelphia man's letter, such as his name, address, date of birth, etc.

"Then, in about ten or fifteen seconds, Cayce began speaking in a slow, carefully worded voice that sounded a bit different in quality from his normal speaking voice. Perhaps the best description of it is the tone of voice one uses when trying hard to recall some far-off fact that has almost slipped out of memory. He repeated the facts given in the letter, slowly, word for word. Then, starting with the present date, he mentioned several dates, going backward in time until he arrived at the date of the man's birth, which I believe was in 1897. Following this, Cayce addressed himself to the man's past background, more or less in terms of generalities.

"The man, in one of his past selves, had been a cheap politician. There was some condemnation of him for not living up to the highest he knew, of being pig-headed and self-centered. Much of it was an urge to the man that he change his course of life from selfishness to unselfishness, from being concerned about his own desires to making himself helpful to others, and that he be true to himself and his God. It had all the earmarks of preaching about it.

"At the end of twenty-five or thirty minutes of this, Cayce said, 'Questions?' Whereupon Mrs. Cayce read off several questions the man wanted answered. In a more straightforward manner than previously, Cayce answered the man's questions one by one. Then he said, 'That's all.' At this point, Mrs. Cayce read the usual formula: that the body now will resume its former functions, that in a short time it will wake up and be none the worse for the wear, or words to that effect.

"In about half a minute, Cayce woke up with the appearance of wondering what had happened while he was in the trance. Mrs. Bro spoke words of surprise at some of the things brought out in the reading and Cayce put on his tie and coat and went into the next room, possibly to get himself something to eat, since I understand he usually takes a glass of milk and a cracker after one of his readings.

"The session had had its interesting aspects, but I was somewhat disappointed in the contents of the life reading. It contained few specifics, and practically all the factual information had been so vague and general in its application that it could have applied to almost anybody. The special significance of the session for me, however, was that for the first time in my life I had observed trance mediumship. What had heretofore been left to the domain of fortune-tellers and cheap magicians, I now observed carried out with dignity and reverence by a body of sensible and sincere people who not only believed that it was possible to secure information in extrasensory ways but were conscientiously engaged in doing it.

"I felt a sense of gratitude for the hospitality of this unusual family which had graciously opened up its home to a stranger and made it possible for me to know them intimately. Following the afternoon reading, I spent an hour talking with Mrs. Cayce and others. I left with just time enough to catch the bus back to the hotel in Norfolk, where I hurriedly snatched my grips and caught the ferry to Cape Charles en route to New York."

During my stay at Virginia Beach, Cayce had generously offered to give me a life reading as a ministerial courtesy, for which he never accepts remuneration. I eagerly accepted his offer, but because of his crowded schedule, booked up two years in advance, it was necessary to set the date a considerable time in the future. To my regret, the appointment never took place. At the time it fell due, because of Cayce's failing health, the doctor had ordered him to give no more readings but to take a much needed rest. He died shortly thereafter at the age of sixty-seven. Earlier, in confirming the appointment, Cayce wrote to me the following personal letter, which reveals the generous, helpful spirit of the man:

"It was indeed a great pleasure to have you come in and see us. . . . I only trust that we may be the means of a real service to you. I am sure you know, I do not want to be the 'blind leading the blind.' Whether the appointment for your life reading and information presented might be just that or not, I do not know. . . . I am sure conviction and faith must come from our own spiritual experiences and all by the grace of God. But that we have found good, we present with the hopes that others may find good and they may apply it in their own experiences. . . . I trust that you will find your ministry there a wonderful field of work and that you may have within yourself, to give to others, that which will point the way to Jesus, the Christ."

A few weeks after our arrival in the Northeast, Cayce came to New York City for a lecture, which we attended. The auditorium was so crowded that it was necessary for us to attend the second lecture. Cayce had agreed to come only on the condition that no one present would attempt to make a date for a reading. I quote from a letter I wrote to a friend, describing the meeting.

"I was really proud of Cayce. He gave a sure enough sermon to one of the most fed-up groups of people I have seen for many a day. Seemingly, like the Greeks of ancient Athens, they had come to 'tell and hear some new thing,' doubtless expecting some occult demonstrations of magic, and not counting on what they got. My guess is that many of them had not been to church or synagogue since they were children. It seemed almost to take away their breath when Cayce bowed his head just before speaking and said, 'Let us pray.' He then prayed a short but impressive prayer, which seemed to change that atmosphere considerably.

"Cayce said very little about his work but spoke to them along the line of treating their fellow man justly, of stopping their hating, and of letting God do his work of grace in their hearts. In such an atmosphere, we were made to realize how fundamentally sound he was in his sense of values. It was plain that he was not seeking something for himself; instead, his Christian faith and generous spirit of helpfulness came out in all he said. Cayce jokingly remarked that he had never before been able to get crowds like this one to listen to him. He said the trouble had always been that even though he said much more important things when he was awake than when asleep, people would listen to him while he was asleep, but not when he was awake. We shook hands with him at the close and told him we thought New York City needed more of his preaching. He laughed heartily at that."

My visit to Virginia Beach was my first encounter with people who seriously accept the doctrine of reincarnation. The average American has been casually aware that the idea of rebirth is a component part of certain Eastern religions, particularly those of India, but my meeting with the Cayce family was the first time I had ever met anyone who regarded the idea as a viable option of thought. Since the time of my visit, and to a great extent because of the Edgar Cayce writings, the concept of reincarnation has become familiar to most Americans. A considerable number of them, however, are badly mixed up as to its real meaning and often confuse the idea with the Christian doctrine of the Incarnation or the belief in human survival after death.

Since Cayce's death, a considerable amount of work has been conducted by psychiatrists and parapsychologists in age regression, the process of apparently moving, in memories, backward in time. This work has strengthened the case for reincarnation and added to its plausibility. In deep hypnotic states, certain individuals can be taken back into memories and recollections of early life, childhood, infancy and, in some instances, to purported previous lifetimes, as in the widely publicized case in *The Search for Bridey Murphy* by Morey Bernstein.[1]

Bernstein's book, dealing with the author's experiments in age regression, was published in 1956. It originated as a result of a previous contact with Cayce. Bernstein, a young Colorado lawyer and amateur hypnotist, set out to expose Cayce as a fraud. After visiting with him at Virginia Beach, however, and examining Cayce's work there, Bernstein decided to use hypnosis to look for evidence of previous lives. Eventually, he found among his acquaintances a young woman, Mrs. Virginia Tighe, who in deep trance state reverted to

---

1   Morey Bernstein, *The Search for Bridey Murphy* (Garden City, N.Y. Doubleday, 1956).

speaking of a life in Ireland that seemed so authentic as to suggest reincarnation. *The Denver Post* sent one of its feature writers to Ireland to try to verify the existence of Bridey Murphy. What this writer found was baffling and inconclusive, but still difficult to dismiss as pure fiction or imagination.

Much of the reincarnationist literature that has flooded the newsstands and bookstores in recent years accepts the idea of rebirth as a proven fact. But the truth of the matter is that reincarnation is only one of several possible explanations of Cayce's life readings. There are alternate theories that could prove to be equally valid.

Indeed, both of Cayce's sons believe that their father's sources of information for previous lives may have included one or more of the following: (1) unconscious memory, things he knew consciously but had forgotten; (2) telepathic communication between their father's sub-conscious or superconscious mind and that of other individuals; and (3) clairvoyant observation obtained by travel out of his own body or similar extrasensory means. Other researchers of the psychic are inclined to believe that "possession," temporarily, of the living by deceased entities, not reincarnation, is the more likely explanation of age-regression material.

Probably the most sizeable body of work conducted to date in this area has been carried on by Dr. Ian Stevenson of the University of Virginia School of Medicine, in Charlottesville, who has investigated numerous examples of persons who claim to remember a previous life. In a little brochure, called *The Evidence for Survival from Claimed Memories of Former Incarnations*, Dr. Stevenson analyzes twenty-eight examples of persons who gave evidence of one sort or another that they had previously lived on the earth. In fact, in these cases it was possible to identify the remembered person and to show that the facts "remembered" matched in six or more items the facts of the deceased person's life.

Although Dr. Stevenson has probably done more work in this field than any other contemporary researcher, he does not claim that the evidence is conclusive, only that the idea appears reasonable. He writes, "I will say, therefore, that I think reincarnation the most plausible hypothesis for understanding the cases of this series. This is not to say that I think they prove reincarnation, either singly or together. Indeed, I am quite sure they do not."

Students of Edgar Cayce's writings frequently accept the doctrine of reincarnation as a matter of faith and become quite dogmatic in their position. Yet Cayce himself never claimed that what came through his mediumship was unadulterated truth. Indeed, he was too humble for that. His own experience led him to recognize that psychic phenomena are often "colored" by the subconscious of the sensitive and, at best, represent a mixture of truth and error.

In evaluating the two aspects of Cayce's mediumship, Dr. Stevenson regards the health readings as being distinctively superior to the life readings and says, "The evidence for Edgar Cayce's clairvoyance regarding current features of living persons and their affairs seems to me to be extremely strong and that for the verifiability of his life readings extremely weak." Yet even the health readings, as Dr. Stevenson recognized, were far from being 100 percent correct.

As we have previously noticed, Cayce himself had misgivings as to the accuracy of his readings, even to the end of his life. At the time of my visit in 1943, two years before his death, I got the impression that Cayce still lived with a wholesome doubt in his mind about the matter, that perhaps, after all, the information regarding reincarnation he received during his trance experiences might be faulty and had its origin in an early blow to his head, a quirk in the brain, or some other undetermined reason.

While there are certain plausible reasons that are supportive of the concept of reincarnation, there are others equally strong against the doctrine. Many people are willing to accept the validity of the Edgar Cayce phenomenon in respect to his health readings who would part company with him over his concept of reincarnation. Dr. James H. Hyslop, formerly professor of ethics and logic at Columbia University, a convinced survivalist who spent more than a quarter of a century studying psychic phenomena, presents two important objections to the reincarnation hypothesis when he says:

"What is it that can recommend the doctrine of reincarnation to its believers is difficult to understand. It contains nothing desirable and nothing ethical. Reincarnation is not desirable, because it does not satisfy the only instinct that makes survival of any kind interesting, namely the instinct to preserve the consciousness of personal identity. . . . Man's only interest in survival is for the persistence of his personal identity. A future life must be the continuity of his consciousness or it is not a life to us at all.

"Moreover, there is nothing ethical in the doctrine. The absolutely fundamental condition of ethics is memory and the retention of personal identity, and memory and personal identity are excluded from the process of reincarnation. That you cannot maintain a theory of responsibility in any existence without memory is a truism in ethics and even in our civil courts. If personal identity were changed, we could not be held responsible for anything we did."

The distinguished English philosopher, Professor C. D. Broad, in his *Lectures on Physical Research* added his objection to accepting the doctrine when he said, "There is not the faintest empirical evidence to suggest that reincarnation, if it happens at all, is anything but an extremely rare and exceptional occurrence." It is evident that while it lacks sufficient evidence at this stage of the game to be regarded as an established fact, the concept of reincarnation will remain as a working hypothesis with psychical researchers for a long time to come.

In the years following my visit with Edgar Cayce, I have met a host of persons with very positive views on the subject of reincarnation. Some of these held strongly, and often dogmatically, to the concept of rebirth, while others found the idea distasteful. My personal position, after years of study and wide human contacts in the paranormal field, is a tentative judgment in the matter. I do not affirm it as a fact, nor deny it as a matter of possibility. In this respect, as in all other aspects of psychic phenomena, a healthy skepticism is an absolute necessity, and so is an open mind.

three

Psychologically Gifted Persons I Met in New Jersey

My initial meeting with Edgar Cayce proved to be the beginning of a quest that has continued to the present time, eventually carrying me on far journeys to various parts of the world. From this point on, and almost as if by magic, circumstances began to open up additional contacts that had never seemed possible before. Shortly after our arrival in New Jersey, I met a man who had wide interests and experience in psychic investigation, Dr. Sherwood Eddy himself.

I first heard Dr. Eddy lecture to a group of students while I was in my senior year at college and had been greatly impressed by him. He was one of the founders of the World Christian Student Movement and, along with Dr. John R. Mott and Dr. Robert E. Speer, made up a triumvirate of Christian leadership that was widely known and greatly admired by the college generation of that day.

As the all-Asia executive secretary of the Young Men's Christian Association (YMCA), Dr. Eddy became a friend and associate of many of the intellectual and political leaders of the world, including Gandhi, Nehru, Woodrow Wilson, Lloyd George, Clement Attlee, Chiang Kai-shek, and others of the world's notables. It was estimated that more people in the Orient had heard him speak than had heard any other Westerner.

Some months after our arrival in New Jersey, Dr. Eddy made a lecture tour of the churches of the New York area under the sponsorship of the National Council of Churches. I was quick to invite him as a guest speaker for my congregation. On the agreed date, I picked him up at his New York apartment and drove him back to New Jersey for the lecture.

I found him forceful and full of energy, a rapid-fire talker and so widely traveled and informed on world affairs that it seemed there was hardly a place he had not been nor any key intellectual or political figure of the world that he did not know personally, in many cases intimately. I had by no means forgotten the letter (mentioned in chapter 1) that Dr. Eddy had written me several years before concerning his psychic experiences. I was eager to discuss it with him. When we eventually got around to it, he responded with genuine enthusiasm and began to talk on the subject with the eagerness of a boy who had been admitted to membership on the team or of a crusader on a fresh trail.

As we drove through the heavy New York traffic, I listened in rapt attention as Dr. Eddy told how, in his wide travels in America, Britain, India, and the Far East, he had had intimate contact with variously gifted persons who were in touch with two worlds, the visible and the invisible. Such persons were carrying on active communication in much the same way nuclear physicists were exploring the atom. He was convinced that through some of these psychically endowed people, he had been in direct contact with members of his own family on the Other Side.

Dr. Eddy had become convinced of the need for additional proof of life after death as a result of his speaking to thousands of British and American soldiers during World War I. As for himself, he said he had always held a belief in eternal life on the grounds of his Christian faith, and this faith had been sufficient, but that there are millions of people who do not have this faith.

Civilians can often ignore the question, but the soldiers to whom he spoke were avid for evidence, especially on the eve of battle. "If I had three nights with a battalion in France before it left for the front," Dr. Eddy said, "I would take as my subject, 'Over the Top and After: or Death and What Lies Beyond.' At that time, I knew nothing about the subject of survival from an empirical standpoint, and I had no scientific evidence to offer the men, but heart-hungry before entering battle, they always crowded that third meeting."

Years later, after he himself had obtained scientific evidence to give them, Dr. Eddy found the same response as he spoke to young aviators training in World War II. They eagerly asked him questions and wondered why they had not been told such things before. Many of them could not sleep all night as they discussed together the pressing question of a future life, of special importance to air pilots, who had the largest mortality rate of any branch of the service. Also, he had found the same eager desire for further proof to sustain a feeble faith among relatives and friends who had lost loved ones in the war, or in the period following.

Dr. Eddy's active quest for an answer to whether there is actually scientific evidence to support a rational belief in personal immortality or whether such a belief is purely a matter of blind religious faith did not begin until 1937. At that time, a devout Quaker friend of his, Edward C. Wood of Philadelphia, felt a "concern" to ask him to investigate psychic evidence for survival and gave him some books to read on the subject. Wood told Dr. Eddy that he knew of a few highly sensitive individuals in touch with both worlds who could furnish him with the direct evidence of the survival of human personality after death. Shortly thereafter, he introduced Dr. Eddy to some of these gifted persons.

As a result of this introduction, Dr. Eddy began an unhurried exploration of the metaphysical field in connection with his other interests and engagements throughout the world. Setting out with no psychic abilities himself, he traveled on three continents seeking out sensitives of outstanding reputation and keeping records of all the evidence he received. He said he considered himself particularly fortunate in coming in touch with some of the most powerful psychics and of being preserved from the painful ordeal of fakes and frauds, of which he had a horror.

Dr. Eddy's years of investigation brought him in touch with "a great cloud of witnesses" to personal immortality. Among the earlier ones whom he encountered in his search were the well-known American sensitive Arthur Ford; Mrs. Pamela Nash, the noted London trance medium; the English psychic healer W. T. Parish; and Edgar Cayce, with whom he spent three days at Virginia Beach. Other friends and coinvestigators in the field of research were Gardner Murphy, the distinguished psychologist of Columbia University; the novelist Upton Sinclair and his psychic wife, whose joint experiments were recorded in their book *Mental Radio*;[1] Betty and Stewart Edward White; Ozora Davis, president of Chicago Theological

---

1   Upton Sinclair, *Mental Radio* (Springfield, Ill.: C. C. Thomas, 1962).

Seminary, a man who had many psychic experiences; the Duke University investigators William McDougall and J. B. Rhine; and British Air Chief Lord Dowding, who directed the Battle of Britain against Hitler's overwhelming air force and who once told Eddy about his own convincing psychic experiences and after-death contacts with some of his beloved airmen who had been shot down.

Dr. Eddy spent more than twelve years collecting and evaluating the evidence of the life beyond, evidence he received through sensitives and researchers sought out in the course of his travels in many countries. In the end, he condensed the results in his book *You Will Survive after Death*.[1] Although he had previously written thirty books in a variety of important areas, including such public issues as war and peace, social and economic justice, and personal religious values, he regarded this last book as his most important.

Dr. Eddy went on to say that during the past several years, with one or two exceptions, his experience of psychic phenomena had been so repeated, so convincing, and so satisfying to him personally that he now felt he had the same evidence in principle for the existence of the seven members of his family who are now in the spiritual world as he had for the five members still on earth. "My belief in personal immortality," he said, "was once a matter of faith; now, it is faith plus knowledge."

I did not realize when I drove Dr. Eddy back to his apartment in New York City that shortly thereafter we would be meeting in frequent association, a pattern that would continue until his death. A few weeks before our

---

1 . Sherwood Eddy, *You Will Survive after Death* (New York: Rinehart, 1950).

initial visit, a book called *Across the Line*, written by Mrs. Anice Terhune of Pompton Lakes, New Jersey, came off the press.[1] I had hardly finished reading it when Dr. Eddy called me from New York to know if I would arrange a conference with Mrs. Terhune for him. He had never met her and was eager to do so. Mrs. Terhune was the widow of the noted author Albert Payson Terhune, famous for his stories of the collies of Sunnybank. Her book, which had been received through automatic writing, contained purported communications received from her husband since his death a few years previously.

Mrs. Terhune had continued to live at their lovely home at Sunnybank after his death. They both had been lovers of dogs and owned a number of splendid collies. When Terhune died, he owed certain people copies of the pedigree of dogs he had sold them. After several days of searching through desk drawers and boxes for the missing papers, Mrs. Terhune became exhausted and was almost in despair. As she stood in her husband's study in abject perplexity as to what to do, a voice suddenly spoke to her and said, "Look behind you, little girl. They're right there!" She then turned and opened one of the cabinet drawers she had previously gone through. There at the center of a large bundle of letters she found the missing papers. She was overjoyed, because she felt that her husband was alive and helping.

Some months later, during a Maundy Thursday evening church service, Mrs. Terhune was thinking of her husband's grave in the church cemetery just outside and silently began to weep. Suddenly, she looked up and saw a light moving near the church ceiling, then coming

---

1   Anice Morris Terhune, *Across the Line* (New York: The Dryden Press, 1945).

closer to her. As it descended, she said it became the face and form of her husband. His eyes looked steadily into hers for a few minutes and then he vanished. Later, she asked her pastor whether he had noticed anything unusual during the service. He had not, he replied, but he had seen her face and knew at once that she had seen a vision.

I readily arranged the meeting as Dr. Eddy requested, and the day following his call, we drove the forty miles to Pompton Lakes for our visit with Mrs. Terhune. A white-haired, soft-spoken lady of unmistakable culture and intelligence, she welcomed us cordially into her home. For more than two hours, we discussed her experiences.

Her opening remark, after we had been seated, was to the effect that there was something strikingly significant in our visit that she must tell us about. In one of the messages she had received from her husband, he had told her to "get Sherwood Eddy" to write the foreword of her book. "Dr. Eddy," she said, "I am ashamed to say it, but at the time I received the message I had never heard of you. I had to look you up in *Who's Who* in order to know who you were." She then went on to relate how she had tried to get in touch with Dr. Eddy during the time of his wife's fatal illness but was unable to reach him. For this reason, she had asked Dr. Joseph Sizoo, pastor of Collegiate Church in New York, to write the foreword. "Isn't it strange," she added, "that you should be coming to see me now?"

Mrs. Terhune related a number of unusual experiences she had had since the book was written. She said that before her husband's death, neither of them had given any mind to psychic matters but that in her bereavement she had become interested. Through a friend who had the gift of automatic writing, she herself had developed the power. Twice, Mrs. Terhune said, she had been able to see her husband since his death. Once he materialized in a chair before her for a few minutes.

In addition, Mrs. Terhune told us how she had been warned in one of the messages she had received that a neighbor friend was contemplating suicide and that she must try to dissuade him from doing so without letting him know where she had gotten the information. When she asked how she could do so without giving away the secret, her husband informed her that the opportunity would soon arise. Within a day or so, the friend came over for a brief visit and let out that he was planning to do just what had been feared. In the course of this and later conversations, she was able to dissuade him. At that time, the issue seemed to have been happily settled.

I inquired about her experience of finding the pedigrees, whether she actually heard the words or whether they were only mental impressions. She stated that the words themselves seemed to have been actually uttered as indicated. Had someone else been present, she felt he probably would have heard nothing, but the words came to her as words and not merely as ideas. I also asked her about the Maundy Thursday service in the church. She described the vision she had there as being more objective and tangible than a mere mental image. Mrs. Terhune had the impression for those moments that she was looking upon something outward and genuinely real, although, of course, she, at the time, knew it to be something that she alone saw.

I was curious to know her technique of automatic writing. She said that it was as though something were pushing the pencil along and she was simply holding it. Frequently, she said, she did not know what was written until she read the page. After her book was finished, her husband suggested that she not continue to do automatic writing since it would prove to be a strain on her physical strength. Instead, she now goes apart at a set time each day and receives his messages by mental impression. A twitching of her left hand is an indication of his presence.

I asked her how she could distinguish between her own thoughts and those that came from her husband. She replied that she knew they were not hers because he told her things she did not know.

As I sat listening to Mrs. Terhune, I found myself thinking how the public generally would regard what she was saying. It would be looked upon as sheer fantasy, if not something more serious. Yet it was easy to see that if she believed anything, she believed what she was relating. Furthermore, the character and intelligence of the woman gave it weight and set us wondering. If she is off the beam, who is sane? If she and others who have had similar experiences lack sanity, then it would appear that our most intelligent people cannot be trusted. We left Mrs. Terhune's home wishing we could have remained longer.

A few months later, I visited the noted researcher Dr. J. B. Rhine (1895–1980), director of the parapsychology laboratory at Duke University. During our summer vacation, my wife and I and our two teenage children drove to Durham, North Carolina, to meet the man whose experimental work had made his name a household word for many people.

Dr. Rhine generously gave us a couple of hours of his time. We asked questions and heard him relate some of his interesting experiments in the field of extrasensory perception, or ESP. We found him to be a friendly, sensitive person who exercised extreme scientific caution. He said that his work at Duke shows that the ancient and accepted doctrine of science, the belief that nothing can enter the mind except through the gateway of the recognized senses, must now give way to a new frontier of the mind.

At the time of our visit with Dr. Rhine, many of the physical scientists looked on his experimental results in telepathy and ESP with disbelief and even ridicule. In the years that have followed, however, telepathy has generally come to be accepted as a fact by the public as well as by many important figures in the scientific establishment itself.

Unquestionably, Dr. Rhine's careful, painstaking work has had a wide influence in producing this change and making psychic research academically respectable. An even greater reason for the change, however, is the modified view of the universe and the new conception of the dynamic nature of matter brought about by the work of theoretical physicists, particularly through the massive influence of Dr. Albert Einstein, the great mathematician. His views of the universe have revolutionized the thought of mankind.

On our return home from Durham, we stopped at the School for Advanced Studies on the campus of Princeton University in New Jersey for a brief visit with Dr. Einstein—a visit I have ever since regarded as one of the most memorable encounters of my life. A unique and fortunate circumstance made the visit possible and gave us the opportunity of a close-up impression of the mysterious and awesome figure whose monumental equation (energy equals mass multiplied by the square of the speed of light) has since become as imposing a thing in scientific circles as the Ten Commandments of Moses is to the Judeo-Christian ethic.

Ushered into his study, we found Dr. Einstein to be an impressive individual with long white hair, full oval face, and large luminous eyes. The overall impression of his personality was that of a childlike spirit with a profound and humane mind. My introduction to the Einstein mystique had occurred years before in a physics class in college, where I first heard of his theory of relativity. At that time, I had the impression that if I were ever lucky enough to meet the great man, his intellectual brilliance would sweep me off my feet.

But to my surprise, when actually in his presence, it was not his intellect that most impressed me, but the gentle, humble spirit of the man. Never have I been in the presence of a person whose unassuming modesty and humility were more evident. I had met the cocksure, dogmatic scientist, but here was a person of a different sort, one who could say with Thomas Huxley, the great nineteenth-century biologist, "Sit down before the facts as a little child, be prepared to give up every preconceived notion, and follow humbly wherever nature leads or you will learn nothing."

The clothes Einstein wore were as unpretentious as the man. They consisted of khaki trousers with suspenders, a cotton shirt open at the collar, and a pair of leather sandals. He could easily have been mistaken for one of the workmen about the building. One incident particularly revealed the humble spirit of the man. In the course of our conversation, we referred to the lady who had ushered us in from the adjoining room as "your secretary." He quickly corrected us by saying, "Not mine!" and then with a wave of hand, "She is ours! She's for all of us on this floor."

During our conversation with Dr. Einstein, we remarked that he resembled pictures we had seen of Dr. Albert Schweitzer, the great African missionary. He responded by saying that Dr. Schweitzer was a dear friend of his and that many people, including a lady whom he had met some months before on the train, had mistaken him for Dr. Schweitzer. It seemed to us, however, that the similarity between the two great men was deeper than mere physical resemblance. There was something in the spiritual quality of Einstein that was strikingly similar to Dr. Schweitzer's "reverence for life"—a reverence on the part of Dr. Schweitzer for all living things that made him unwilling to destroy the smallest creature and caused him to treat every human being with the profoundest respect. Indeed, the truly great are the gentle, compassionate people.

At the time of our visit, Dr. Einstein was attempting to find one grand unified field theory that would encompass causality in the cosmos from galaxies to the inside of the atom. In the course of our conversation, we referred to the modified concept of the universe that his work had brought about, and I asked him if the new physics had been able to forecast some master design, or ultimate goal, toward which the universe might be moving. He responded by saying that human intelligence can only grasp a tiny segment of total reality. The cosmos is so vast and mysterious and our knowledge is so inadequate that he did not think it possible to say whether creation does or does not have an ultimate goal.

The subject of psychic investigation did not come up in the course of our visit with Dr. Einstein. We naturally assumed that since he was a theoretical physicist and not a psychologist, he would probably have little if any concern for that field of research. In fact, the very idea that the greatest living example of pure science could have had an interest in the study of psychic phenomena would have scandalized the orthodox establishment of that day. However, we were later to learn that, while Dr. Einstein himself doubtless never engaged in psychic research, he did have an open mind and sympathetic interest in the subject. On one occasion, when asked his opinion concerning metaphysical phenomena, he is on record as saying, "It is possible that there exist human emanations which are still unknown to us. Do you remember how electrical and 'unseen waves' were laughed at? The knowledge of man is still in its infancy."

Also, at the time when most physical scientists scoffed at such things as telepathy and ESP, Dr. Einstein had written an introduction to the German edition of Upton Sinclair's *Mental Radio*, in which he expressed appreciation for the quality of Sinclair's work in the following terms: "In no case should the psychologically interested pass over this book without heed. . . . The results of the telepathic experiments carefully and plainly set forth in it stand far beyond those which a nature investigator holds to be thinkable. On the other hand, it is out of the question in the case of so conscientious an observer and writer as Upton Sinclair that he is carrying on a conscious deception of the reading world; his good faith and dependability are not to be doubted."

It is evident from the above that Dr. Einstein was not the kind of a person who would regard the investigation of psychic phenomena as cheap and future nonsense, as so many intellectually lesser physical scientists have done. Indeed, more than any other scientist in our contemporary world, Einstein brought out the truth that the invisible is the truly real, that whatever the senses can perceive are phenomena, merely, and that all the energies and realities of the universe are and forever remain invisible.

He is quoted as saying: "Anyone who studies physics deeply enough is inevitably led to metaphysics. . . . The most beautiful and profound emotion we can experience is the sensation of the mystical. It is the sower of all true science. He to whom this emotion is a stranger, who can no longer wonder and stand rapt in awe, is as good as dead. To know that what is impenetrable to us really exists, manifesting itself as the highest wisdom and the most radiant beauty which our dull faculties can comprehend only in their most primitive forms—this knowledge, this feeling is at the center of true religion."

The man who wrote the preceding paragraph was no arrogant, self-opinionated person, but a humble man in touch with transcendent reality. There was a priceless quality about our visit with Dr. Einstein, and we left for home feeling that we had not only met a great scientist but also a great man.

Another great contemporary mystic whom we later met was Dr. Frank C. Laubach,[1] the originator of the World Campaign for Christian Literacy, a man whom Norman Cousins[2] called "one of the noblest human beings of our time." Dr. Laubach had become known as "the Apostle of Literacy" because of his prodigious labors among the 1.2 billion adult illiterates of the human family. Through his simplified method of "each one teach one," he and his helpers had enabled more than 100 million adults, speaking 200 different languages, to read and write.

I first learned of him by reading his little book, *Letters of a Modern Mystic*, a priceless gem of devotion comparable to any of the other great spiritual classics, such as *Theologia Germanica* or Brother Lawrence's *The Practice of the Presence of God*.[3] It was evident to me on reading the book that here was one of the great mystics of modern times, a man whose extensive practical labors sprang out of a prayer life far beyond the ordinary.

---

1   Frank C. Laubach, American educator and missionary (1884–1970).

2   Norman Cousins, American educator and essayist (1912–90).

3   Frank Laubach, Letters of a Modern Mystic (Westwood, N.J.: Revell, 1958); Der Franckforter, *Theologia Germanica* (New York: Pantheon, 1949); Brother Lawrence, *The Practice of the Presence of God* (New York: Paulist Press, 1978).

I first met Dr. Laubach when he spoke in our church, after which he and his wife were overnight visitors in our home. St. Francis of Assisi had the ability to love everybody, including the birds and animals and sun and moon, and make them feel that he did. It was this impression our guests inspired in us: gentleness, genuineness, and an outflowing love for all created persons and things.

Much of our conversation had to do with Dr. Laubach's practice and experience of prayer. We were not surprised to find that he had a firm belief in telepathy and was in the habit of practicing it. Indeed, he recognized that prayer is essentially directed thought and, in itself, is a telepathic process. Proof of this, he said, is the fact that when we pray, we do not write God a letter or call him over the telephone or shout at him to make him hear us. Instead, we project our thoughts toward him in mental conversation. Communion with God is therefore the interaction of personal minds—the mind of man and the mind of God—in conscious awareness and communication with each other.

This is not to suggest that prayer is only telepathy, or that psychic and spiritual realities are identical, but they do overlap and have similar basic qualities. Just as the joyous fellowship of a meal with friends is more than digestion, so prayer is much more than telepathy, but it is telepathy and has telepathic qualities.

As might be expected, Dr. Laubach was in complete agreement with Alfred, Lord Tennyson, who said, "More things are wrought by prayer than this world dreams of." Dr. Laubach felt that we had pursued scientific inquiry in many directions, with spectacular results, but that we have failed to investigate and use the mighty energies that prayer can release. Since the world at any one moment is the result of the total thought forces that struggle for supremacy, prayer can be the solution to many of the world's problems. By it, we can help God to accomplish what he wants done in the world.

Dr. Laubach told us that groups under his leadership have organized prayer broadcasts for key individuals in public life, with significant results. He felt that we can often do more for the world through prayer than if we could walk into offices of leaders in London, Moscow, or Washington and tell them what to do. Our advice to them might be faulty, but if they listened to God, they could not go wrong.

Dr. Laubach thought that if ten million people prayed with systematic earnestness, stopping for a few seconds every five or ten minutes each day to flash a prayer at the president, congressmen, members of the United Nations, and other world leaders, the effect could be incalculable. Our prayers could thus become a potent factor in influencing such persons to make their day-by-day decisions in keeping with God's will. In fact, every prayer we utter from the heart, he believes, begins to change history.

Dr. Laubach's personal method of prayer is similar to that of Brother Lawrence's. His technique is known as "the game with minutes," which is the practice of recalling God to mind as frequently as possible throughout the day. This method includes two special features to guide those who would practice it:

1. You have hitherto thought of God for only a few seconds or minutes a week, and he was out of your mind the rest of the time. Now you are attempting, like Brother Lawrence, to practice the presence of God and keep God in mind each minute you are awake.

2. As you practice praying for people in a crowd, try to see double, as Christ does—to see the person as he is and the person Christ longs to make of him. Remarkable things happen and the atmosphere of

a room changes when a few people keep whispering a prayer about the rest.

Dr. Laubach said he thinks perhaps there is no finer ministry than to be in meetings or crowds, whispering the name of Jesus, and then helping people whenever we see an opportunity. He himself is in the habit of praying for people behind their heads as he rides on trains and buses and watching them eventually betray their awareness of his mental broadcast through certain responses they make. Some act as if they had been spoken to or show other signs of being "tuned in," such as putting their head in their hands, looking upward and closing their eyes, or oftentimes speaking to him. Once he was praying for a woman in front of him on the train. Out of the blue, for no apparent reason, the woman turned around and broke the silence by saying, "What the world needs is more religion."

On another occasion, he was sitting in a railway station praying for the people around him. One of the men kept looking at him as though to ask, "Did you speak to me?" A young woman nearby whispered something to her soldier friend, and he replied aloud, "You're just psychic, that's all." Both of these persons were looking hard at Dr. Laubach. "It must be the prayer that does it," said our guest, "for when I do not pray for people they usually show neither interest nor friendliness, but the moment the prayer pressure starts, the strange sweet kindliness begins to appear on people's faces and they look at me ready to talk."

There were instances he had known, Dr. Laubach said, where prayer became so intense, so charged with love and concern, that he had seen it transmuted into psychokinesis, or the action of mind on matter. In addressing Christian congregations, he often requested that they pray for him as he talked. The results always proved to be good, and in some cases marvelous. In his book, *Prayer, the Mightiest Force in the World*, Dr. Laubach relates a striking incident of this sort that took place at a Camp Farthest Out when a large group of people became one in prayer.[1]

As the group prayed in intensity and harmony, the speaker seemed to be possessed by Christ and felt as if Christ were talking through his lips. Six people came to him at the close of the service and said, "We saw Christ standing by you." As he went out of the church, a woman was sobbing with her head on the seat, and when he spoke to her, she said, "I don't believe in such things, but what can I do? I saw Christ myself." In this case, it would seem that the audience was so melded into one by prayer that it had in some way enabled the invisible Christ to become visible to about a dozen eyes.

At another time, in a large open-air meeting in Denver, something as solid as steel seemed to come up out of the group of praying people. An invisible something gripped the speaker's arms and he involuntarily grasped the table in front of him. The next moment it lay shattered on the floor and the microphone had been knocked over. It seemed to the speaker that he had not broken the table but that the audience had done it. He picked up the microphone and continued his talk, but that night he lay awake for hours, trembling at the strange thing the audience had done to him.

As we listened to Dr. Laubach describe these and other amazing incidents attributed to the power of prayer, we recalled the description in the Book of Acts of a similar group of whom it was said, "When they had prayed, their meeting place was shaken" (Acts 4:31).

---

1   Frank Laubach, *Prayer, the Mightiest Force in the World* (Westwood, N.J.: Revell, 1959).

A short time after Laubach's visit, I read Alexis Carrel's international best-seller, *Man, the Unknown*.[1] It is significant how the testimony of a great scientist parallels the experience of a great religionist. Dr. Carrel, a Nobel Prize winner and a celebrated medical researcher at the Rockefeller Institute, spent several weeks at the Catholic shrine of Lourdes in France studying reported miracles of healing. He saw many healings of "hysterical" diseases. He witnessed a cancerous sore on a woman's back, which had been there for nine years, shrivel to a scar before his eyes.

Following his experience at Lourdes, Dr. Carrel had this to say about the nature of prayer, a statement in complete accord with all that Dr. Laubach had said on the subject: "Prayer is not only worship, it is also an invisible emanation of man's worshiping spirit—the most powerful form of energy that one can generate. As a physician, I have seen men, after all other therapy had failed, lifted out of disease and melancholy by the serene effort of prayer. It is the only power in the world that seems to overcome the so-called 'laws of nature'; the occasions on which prayer has dramatically done this have been termed 'miracles.' But a constant, quieter miracle takes place hourly in the hearts of men and women who have discovered that prayer supplies them with a steady flow of sustaining power in their daily lives. When we pray, we link ourselves with the inexhaustible motive power that spins the universe."

---

1   Alexis Carrel, *Man, the Unknown* (New York: Harper and Brothers, 1935).

four

More Spiritual Pioneers

My first opportunity to meet psychically gifted individuals and researchers abroad came as a result of a pulpit exchange in the summer of 1950 with a Congregational minister in Birmingham, England. During my four months' stay in Europe, I had the chance to visit a number of persons throughout England, Scotland, and Wales who had special psychic endowments or interests.

The first person I intended to "meet" on my arrival in Britain was a man who had been dead for half a century. I could not afford to overlook the opportunity to pay my respects to Frederic W. H. Myers, the first great pioneer of modern parapsychology and the man whose influence on physical research is comparable to that of Shakespeare on drama. For this reason, shortly after my arrival in Birmingham, I caught the bus to the Lake District of northern England for a visit at the little Anglican Church of St. John's at Keswick, where Myers is buried.

Myers was one of the original founders of the British Society for Psychical Research in 1882, but my first contact with him was not as a psychologist but through his literary masterpiece *St. Paul*, a poem of some hundred and fifty stanzas that has been described as the best interpretation of the soul of the Apostle Paul outside of the New Testament itself.[1]

This poetic gem first cast its spell on me during my college days; in the years that have followed, the haunting cadence of its lines and the spirit of mystic devotion that it breathes have made it one of the priceless literary treasures of my life.

It was years after I first read *St. Paul* that I learned of Myers's important work in psychic research. Although he began his career as a brilliant classical scholar, a poet, and a master of prose style, Myers became a psychologist of such a rank that William James termed his theory of the subconscious an epochal development in the history of science. James said that Myers would always be remembered in psychology as "the pioneer who staked out a vast tract of mental wilderness and planted the flag of genuine science upon it."

Myers is noted for two outstanding contributions to parapsychology: (1) his theory of telepathy as one of the basic laws of life—in fact, he coined the word; and (2) his systematic conception of the "subliminal," which today we call the unconscious, as the greater portion of human personality. His 1903 book *Human Personality and Its Survival of Bodily Death* was the first scholarly attempt to classify and describe psychic phenomena and continues to be probably the most important single work in the literature of the paranormal.[2]

---

1   Frederick William Henry Myers, *St. Paul* (London: Macmillan and Co., Ltd., 1919).

2   Frederick William Henry Myers, *Human Personality and Its Survival of Bodily Death* (New York: Longmans, Green, and Co., 1903).

I spent a couple of hours at St. John's Church, where Myers's father had been the first rector, visiting the sanctuary and strolling in its churchyard. The rectory where Frederic was born is near the church; both stand on an eminence overlooking a vast background of lakes and mountains, a scene that is almost breathtaking in its appeal.

Among the significant memorials in the sanctuary was a tablet to Frederic and his wife, Eveleen, that read: "In memory of Frederic William Henry Myers, son of Rev. Frederic Myers, born at Keswick Feb. 6, 1843. Departed this life at Rome, Jan. 17, 1901; buried at Keswick Feb. 13, 1901. He asked life of thee and thou gavest him a long life, even for ever and ever." Significantly, this last sentence, a quotation from Scripture, refers to the passionate desire for evidence of human survival that animated Myers's life.

Myers had a burning interest in the problem of human destiny. His "preoccupation with unseen things" began early in life. This is brought out in the description of an experience he had at the age of six. "The first grief which I remember came from the sight of a dead mole, which had been crushed by a cartwheel in the Borrowdale road. Deeply moved, I hurried back to my mother, and asked her whether the little mole had gone to heaven. Gently and lovingly, but without doubt, she told me that the little mole had no soul, and would not live again. To this day, I remember my rush of tears at the thought of that furry innocent creature, crushed by a danger which I fancied it too blind to see, and losing all joy forever by that unmerited stroke. The pity of it! the pity of it! and the first horror of a death without resurrection rose in my bursting heart."

Myers was a pioneer in the field of psychical research in an era when scientific investigation all round him proceeded in the opposite direction, toward philosophical materialism and determinism. After some years of eager faith expressed in his early poems, he suffered a gradual disillusionment and loss of faith from the skepticism engendered by the new world of impersonal science and evolutionary biology. He sought to find a rational escape from a deadpan, meaningless universe in which human personality was merely a momentary event devoid of general meaning. No man desired proof of cosmic survival more earnestly than he, and no one labored harder to attain it. In his scientific quest for another life, Myers's aim was to discover a basis for the continuity to spend all his life's energy "beating against the walls of the prison-house in case a panel anywhere might yield." From his friend and favorite teacher Henry Sidgwick (a cofounder of the Society for Psychical Research), Myers first had the idea of the possibility of attaining scientific assurance of unseen things. Years later, Myers describes the eventful meeting between the two: "I felt drawn in my perplexities to Henry Sidgwick as somehow my only hope. In a starlight walk which I shall not forget, I asked him, almost with trembling, whether he thought that when Tradition, Intuition, and Metaphysics had failed to solve the riddle of the Universe, there was still a chance that from actual observable phenomena—ghosts, spirits, whatever there might be—some valid knowledge might be drawn as to a World Unseen."

Upon Sidgwick's cautious encouragement, an informal association was formed at Cambridge for the investigation of these phenomena. Myers himself became the moving spirit of this new endeavor. Later he wrote that he was one of "a central group concerned in a great endeavor; the endeavor to pierce, by scientific methods, the world-old, never-penetrated veil. No one more unreservedly than myself has staked his all upon that distant and growing hope."

Myers staked his all upon the chance of learning the actual truth about the destiny of man. It was given to him to feel the full effects of the tide of agnostic materialism of his day, and then, on the very plane of science that had undermined the faith of multitudes, to rediscover the reality of the spiritual world and the certainty of life after death. At the close of his quest he wrote, "My history has been that of a soul struggling into the conviction of its own existence, postponing all else to the question of whether life and love survive the tomb. That condition has at last been granted me."

In answering the criticism of his professional associates that "dabbling" in psychic phenomena disintegrates the critical faculties and makes one a gullible fool, William James used the pragmatic rebuttal "by their fruits ye shall know them," and offers the example of Frederic Myers himself as one who lived exclusively for psychic research and yet "grew stronger in every particular for his devotion to the same inquiries." In *William James on Psychical Research*,[1] James points out that it was noticeable to Myers's friends that his search for psychic evidence of immortality produced a transformation of his character from a person who was "exclusive and intolerant by nature" to one who became "democratic in sympathy, endlessly patient, and above all, happy."

"When a man's pursuit," observed James, "gradually makes his face to shine and grow handsome, you may be sure it is a worthy one."

My next midweek excursion was to Cambridge, where Frederic Myers had lived much of his life, first as a student and then as an elected fellow and classical lecturer

---

1   William James, *William James on Psychical Research* (New York: Viking Press, 1960).

at Trinity College. Eventually, he gave up his position as lecturer to become inspector of schools, a job that paid him a casual living but gave him more time and freedom to pursue his research. Following marriage, Myers and his wife took up their abode at Leckhampton House, which he built with his own hands on the edge of Cambridge and where his three children were born.

My primary purpose in going to Cambridge was to meet Professor Robert Thouless, the widely recognized psychologist of Corpus Christi College. Dr. Thouless has been a leader in British psychical investigations for a number of years and has had an influence on the work in Britain comparable to that of J. B. Rhine in America. He has done extensive investigation in the field, and reports of his major experiments have appeared in the Journal of Parapsychology and in numerous other publications in England and America.

On my arrival at Cambridge, I found Dr. Thouless to be a quiet, unassuming man, pleasant and unacademic in nature, who received me cordially and made me feel at home with him at once. He told me that J. B. Rhine had been with them a few weeks before for a lecture. We spent an enjoyable afternoon and evening together, strolling over the grassy lawns and pleasant nooks of the university areas, discussing his work in parapsychology and other mutual interests.

I found Dr. Thouless to be no less thorough in his experimental work than Rhine but considerably less cautious and concerned about the good opinion of his fellows in orthodox science. He did not hesitate to state his belief in human survival after death and to affirm its importance as an objective of psychical study. I recall a statement he made during our visit that I felt was highly significant. He said he considered the supernatural element an essential in all religions, and then added, "It seems paradoxical that so many modern theologians are turning their backs on the supernatural just at the time when parapsychology is beginning to make it intelligible."

Before leaving Cambridge, I took a taxi to Leckhampton House, where Myers and his wife had lived until his death. The man who now owned the house was a lordly gentleman of sophisticated vintage who laughed at ghosts; in a bored and indifferent manner, he showed me over his grounds and house. He had known Myers personally and seemed to get pleasure in deriding him and his coworkers for being such silly screwballs as to waste their time "ghost hunting." He did not like ghosts, or even people, for that matter. But because of my interest in the place, I ignored the artificiality of his welcome and took advantage of the chance to pay my respects to the original owner of the house for his spiritual contribution to my life.

My next significant meeting, following the Cambridge visit, was with C. S. Lewis, the noted author and professor at Oxford University. Lewis was a Fellow of Magdalen College, Oxford, at the time I met him, but he later became occupant of the Chair of Medieval and Renaissance English Literature at Cambridge, which he held until his death in 1963. At the time of our visit, he was known as the English teacher turned amateur theologian and the author of *The Screwtape Letters*,[1] but his reputation as a writer and theologian was hardly as extensive then as it is today. His books have now become widely known throughout the English-speaking world. The number of his admirers has developed almost into a

---

1   C. S. Lewis, *The Screwtape Letters* (New York: Macmillan, 1982).

cult. His fascinating spiritual autobiography, *Surprised by Joy*, has become a classic with many persons. Others of his books, such as *Miracles*,[1] his outer-space trilogy, and the *Narnia* stories, promise to be read long after many other books have passed into limbo.

I caught the train at Birmingham on a clear spring morning for the two-hour ride through the lovely English countryside to Oxford and arrived at Magdalen College in time for my eleven o'clock appointment with Lewis. He cordially welcomed me into his living quarters, where a small fire was burning in the grate, and made me feel at ease immediately. I found him to be a very unprepossessing individual, ruddy faced and burly, quite informal in manner. His baggy, brown tweed suit hung loosely on him. He might have been taken for almost anything except an author or professor. In fact, he looked more like the man who raked the hay or a Manhattan truck driver than one who has dealings with academic things.

I expressed my gratification for the fact that an English teacher should be writing what I thought to be some of our best theology, and I wondered how he managed so successfully to express abstract philosophical ideas clearly enough for the ordinary person to grasp and enjoy. He said he didn't know, but he guessed it might be because he had to spend so much time tutoring students. "You have to make what you say to college students simple or they won't understand it, you know." He went on to say that he thought no one had any business writing or teaching something that he did not have the ability to put into language clear enough for the average person to understand.

---

1   C. S. Lewis, *Miracles: A Preliminary Study* (New York: Macmillan, 1947).

Our conversation ranged from the poetry of Dante, whom Lewis regarded as the foremost poet of all times, even surpassing Shakespeare, to a discussion of several of Lewis's own writings. I told him that I thought the imagery of *The Great Divorce*,[1] with its busload of ghosts traveling from hell to heaven and being disappointed with what they found on their arrival was superb, and that it was my favorite of his works. To my surprise, he said that it had had the poorest sale of any of his books up to that time; however, in recent years it seems to have had a growing popularity.

We spent some time discussing the subject of psychism and spirit communication. Unlike John Wesley, the eighteenth-century evangelist and founder of Methodism, who had a lifelong interest in psychic matters and would carefully investigate every type of ghost story or supernormal activity coming to his attention, Lewis seemed to lack interest in the field and purposely avoided it. He did not doubt that overt communication between the living and the dead actually took place on occasions, but he thought that it was incompatible with historic Christianity and should be avoided. The weight of Christian tradition, he felt, was against such a practice.

On looking back upon our conversation, I have caught myself wondering if Lewis's distaste for psychic involvement was not a psychological hangover from his unfortunate experience related in *Surprised by Joy*, with the spiritually immature Miss C., the matron of the preparatory school in Wyvern, who herself was foundering in "the mazes of Theosophy, Rosicrucianism, Spiritualism,

---

1   C. S. Lewis, *The Great Divorce* (New York: Macmillan, 1946).

and the whole Anglo-American Occultist tradition." She didn't realize that in Lewis's case the room in which she brought her candle was full of gunpowder.

An interesting sequel to my meeting with Lewis had to do with the phenomenon of spirit manifestation to J. B. Phillips, the noted translator of the New Testament, an event that took place some years after our visit. Shortly after Lewis's death, Phillips described a personal and memorable experience he had in which Lewis had visibly and audibly appeared to him on two separate occasions. It seems that Lewis had been a decisive factor in encouraging Phillips to complete his translation of the New Testament that later made him famous. The "appearances" themselves had come to Phillips at a time of acute spiritual need. The incidents were investigated by the Society for Psychic Research and recorded in the December 1970 issue of their journal, from which the following passage by Phillips is quoted:

> *Many of us who believe in what is technically known as the Communion of Saints must have experienced the sense of nearness, for a fairly short time, of those whom we love soon after they have died. This has certainly happened to me several times. But the late C. S. Lewis, whom I did not know very well, and had only seen in the flesh once, but with whom I had corresponded a fair amount, gave me an unusual experience. A few days after his death, while I was watching television, he "appeared" sitting in a chair within a few feet of me, and spoke a few words which were particularly relevant to the difficult circumstances through which I was passing. He was ruddier in complexion than ever, grinning all over his face and, as the old-fashioned saying has it, positively glowing with health.*
>
> *The interesting thing to me was that I had not been thinking about him at all. I was neither alarmed nor surprised nor, to satisfy the Bishop of Woolwich, did I look*

up to see the hole in the ceiling that he might have made on arrival. He was just there—large as life and twice as natural! A week later, this time when I was in bed reading before going to sleep, he appeared again, even more rosily radiant than before, and repeated to me the same message, which was very important to me at the time. I was a little puzzled by this, and I mentioned it to a certain saintly Bishop who was then living in retirement here in Dorset. His reply was, "My dear J . . . , this sort of thing is happening all the time."

In its investigation of this remarkable case of spirit manifestation, the British society sent a questionnaire to Phillips, asking him to describe more fully the details of the event. His response to a lengthy list of questions was also published in the society's journal. A condensed summary of some of these questions and his answers can help to clarify Phillips's account and throw additional light upon the nature of his experience.

Question: Dr. Phillips, what were the difficult circumstances through which you were passing?

Phillips: They were largely a matter of feeling mental and spiritual depletion as a result of several years of creative work.

Question: Exactly what words were used by the apparition on both occasions?

Phillips: On the first occasion, the words Lewis said to me were, "It's not as difficult as you think, you know," and exactly the same words were used on the second occasion.

Question: You say the first time you saw the apparition you were "neither alarmed nor surprised." Do you not think it strange that you were not surprised by such an unusual occurrence?

Phillips: At the time, being fairly familiar with the thoughts and ideas of the personality of C. S. Lewis, it did not seem at all strange to me that he should become physically visible and audible after his death. Indeed, it was only afterwards, when relating the occurrences to my wife, that it struck me as "odd" at all. I felt more happy than anything else, for his message seemed to me to bear considerable reassurance.

Question: What were your reactions the second time you saw the apparition?

Phillips: The second appearance happened when I was lying in bed reading and he appeared to be sitting near my bedside. He was, as in the first appearance, about four to five feet away from me. In both cases, my attention was drawn to him in much the same way as it would be if my wife had come quietly into the room, taken a seat near me, and I might have said,"Good gracious, I didn't hear you come in." It was as natural as that. As to the time, I should think it was not more than half a minute in either case.

Question: Have you ever had a comparable experience before or since?

Phillips: No, there has never been anything that could be remotely described as visible or audible.

Question: Can you describe in more detail anything about the apparition?

Phillips: On both occasions, Lewis was dressed in rather rough, well-worn tweeds, brown in color. This did not strike me as remarkable at the time until I realized some weeks later that I had never seen him in ordinary clothes. In fact, despite a sporadic correspondence over the years, I had only seen him once before "in the flesh." This was at a service in the church where he was wearing a black cassock. It was several months later when reading a book about him that I learned that it was his habit to wear tweeds. I cannot emphasize too strongly that he was solid and in no way transparent. When I say he glowed, I do not mean that he was illuminated like the rear light of a car, but that he exhibited in a marked, and somewhat enhanced way, exactly what we mean when we say that a fit man is "glowing with health." The voice was his natural voice, but I was listening intently and could not honestly say whether his lips moved or not. His features were the same as I remembered them in life except that any lines of strain or anxiety were lost in what I can only call his grain of joy.

Shortly after Phillips's book *The Ring of Truth* came off the press,[1] I found it necessary to carry on a bit of correspondence with him concerning a world tour seminar my son and I were conducting. In one of my letters, I expressed appreciation for the fact that he had included in his book the account of Lewis's appearance to him, and then I added the following comment:

"I might be forgiven in seeing a bit of humor in the fact that during his earthly life, Lewis rejected the whole matter of spirit communication because he felt that it was not legitimate for a Christian to communicate with those in the spirit life. Now that he himself has entered into the realm of spirit, he seems to have changed his point of view and now finds it permissible to communicate with you. It is plain truth that he has been converted to the transfiguration viewpoint, which definitely states that Christ himself practiced active communication with two of the so-called dead and audibly discussed with them his approaching death at Jerusalem."

Another significant contact I had while overseas was a visit with Britain's distinguished poet Walter de la Mare. I had long been a lover of his poetry and had looked forward with particular interest to meeting the man who almost

---

1   J. B. Phillips, *The Ring of Truth* (New York: Macmillan, 1967).

certainly would have been selected as England's poet laureate had John Masefield not been living at the time.

The outstanding impression one receives from de la Mare's poetry is that of the supernatural, the feeling of a fantastic other world that lies on the edge of our consciousness. Typical of this is his poem, "The Listeners," which the literary critic Louis Untermeyer describes by saying, "What we have here is the effect, the thrill, the overtones, of a ghost story rather than the narrative itself—the less than half-told adventure of some new Childe Roland heroically challenging a heedless universe. Never have silence and black night been reproduced more creepily, nor has the symbolism of man's courage facing the cryptic riddle of life been more memorably expressed."

The evening before my return to New York, I caught a bus in London and, accompanied by a ministerial friend from America, rode to the poet's house in Twickham, some twenty miles south of the city. We were welcomed at the door by his sister, who had lived with him since his wife's death a few years before. Tea was served almost immediately, and for the next two hours our conversation dealt principally with poems, poets, and the techniques of poetry.

We found Mr. de la Mare highly stimulating, friendly and human, with a touch of philosophical mysticism and a quiet, sparkling sense of humor. He had the delightful knack of keeping himself in the background, drawing others into the conversation. He told us that he had made two lecture tours of America some years back and that he had been a long-time friend of the American poet Robert Frost, whom he admired very much and in some ways resembled.

When I told our host that on one occasion I had given his poem, *The Truants*, to an American friend whose little boy had died and that years later the friend spoke of the poem with much gratitude, he seemed deeply touched. We asked him what poem among his poetic babies was his favorite child and his reply was that it was always the last one he was working on.

Perhaps the mystical temperament of de la Mare and the supernatural quality of his verse are best revealed by the remark he made to us as we were leaving to catch the bus back to London. In response to my thanks to him for the significant contribution he had made to the field of poetry, he modestly answered by saying that it would probably surprise most of us if we knew how really little of human creativity comes from within and how much "comes from the Other Side."

We did not have the opportunity of discussing with him what he meant by receiving things from "the Other Side." At the time of our visit, we were quite unaware that our host was psychically gifted and had had numerous supernormal experiences, including significant dreams and spirit visitants in his bedroom. It was several years later that I read his anthology of modern poetry *Behold, This Dreamer!*, in which he discusses the phenomenon of sleep.[1]

In part one to the volume, de la Mare describes the experience of being under an anesthetic, a "drug-induced departure into the unconscious."

"Only twice have I brought back any clear glimpse of the beyond when under the influence of an anesthetic: once, of a bare patch of gravel brilliant with sunshine; and again, of the shelving sandy banks of a slow-moving

---

1   Walter de la Mare, *Behold, This Dreamer! Of Reverie, Night, Sleep, Dream, Lovedreams, Nightmare, Death, the Unconscious, the Imagination, Divination, the Artist, and Kindred Subjects* (New York: Greenwood Press, 1969).

river, tranquil, and strange to me. . . . The river with its shelving banks was suffused with an intense feeling of homesickness. I grieved at having to come away. The dentist's gas may have accounted for the tragic or sentimental tears that were on my cheeks—but hardly for the acute regret at finding that I had been brought to, had been called back. And though it may be merely a deceit of the senses, this coming back certainly suggests a definite journey."

On one of my later trips to Great Britain, I was privileged to have a visit with Miss Geraldine Cummins, one of the most important automatists of this century. She has produced extraordinary scripts dealing with Biblical times that have shed light on numerous puzzling aspects of the New Testament. At the time I visited her in 1963, she was living in London but was spending the summer with her brother, Dr. Robert Cummins, a physician in Cork, Ireland.

Miss Cummins's automatisms are among the most interesting and valuable known in psychic research. She began her writings in 1923, and up to the time of my visit forty years later, she had produced automatically over a million words of outstanding writings. The major achievement of her mediumship is a series of books collectively called *The Scripts of Cleophas* but published as five individual volumes, arranged chronologically under the following titles: *The Scripts of Cleophas, Paul in Athens, The Great Days of Ephesus, I Appeal unto Caesar,* and *When Nero Was Dictator.*[1]

---

1   Geraldine Cummins, *The Scripts of Cleophas* (New York: H. Vinal, Ltd., 1928); Geraldine Cummins, *Paul in Athens* (London: Rider and Co., 1930); Geraldine Cummins, *The Great Days of Ephesus* (London: Rider and Co., 1933); Geraldine Cummins, *I Appeal to Caesar* (London: Psychic Press, 1950).

With a wealth of argument and detail, *The Scripts* describe the dawn of Christianity, the early beginnings of the Christian church, and the trials and vicissitudes of the first Christians. It is said to be based on lost ancient documents and put into its present form by one called Cleophas, ostensibly the spirit of a deceased personality, who was one of the first disciples to blaze the trail for the Christian church.

Normally, Miss Cummins is not a rapid writer and has to work rather laboriously and with many corrections to produce six hundred or seven hundred words in a couple of days. However, in producing *The Scripts of Cleophas* and other automatic writings, the speed she attained was truly remarkable. On one occasion 2,230 words were written without pause in one hour and thirty-eight minutes. At another sitting, lasting an hour and five minutes, 1,750 words were produced. Eminent theologians and other authorities have witnessed the writing of parts of her scripts. On such occasions, the completed sheets were taken from the automatist each day and locked away before she could read what was written, or they were carried home by the observers to be studied at their leisure. Nevertheless, the continuity of the narrative proceeded smoothly the next day.

On my visit to Miss Cummins, I was accompanied by my son and a ministerial friend from America on an overnight boat trip across the Irish Sea to Cork. Since her brother's home where she was staying was a few miles out of the city, we caught a taxi and arrived there in the early afternoon. Miss Cummins, a small, elfin Irish woman in her sixties, was waiting for us in the yard. We spent three hours in interesting conversation with her and found her to be a woman of versatile talents.

In her early years, she had played on the international hockey team for Ireland, was an enthusiastic tennis player, had written several novels and short stories, and had produced plays that had been staged at the famous Abbey Theater. We were impressed by her genuineness and quiet, gentle spirit. With characteristic modesty, she said concerning her voluminous automatic writings, "I was only the secretary. The authors are in eternity."

We found that Miss Cummins had never traveled in Palestine or the area covered by St. Paul in his journeys, nor had she ever studied theology or Christian origins. It was evident that her knowledge of the New Testament and church history was quite limited. Yet her *Scripts of Cleophas* often give important clues to the solution of Biblical puzzles that she was not aware even existed. I pointed out how her book *I Appeal unto Caesar* had given me a clue to the perplexing question of how Paul had wealth enough to pay the court cost of an appeal to Caesar and yet had mentioned several times in his letters the necessity of working with his hands to make his living. She was amazed at what I told her. It was plain that the problem had never been brought to her attention before.

As a practicing physician in Cork, Miss Cummins's brother was sympathetically interested in his sister's work. Frequently he called on her for help in diagnosing some of his medical cases. Others who have come to her for advice have included not only medical practitioners but clergymen, scientists, and politicians. She told us that Mackenzie King, the prime minister of Canada, had sought her help a number of times. On one occasion, while in London, he had become seriously ill and sent her an urgent request that she and her household companion, Miss Gibbes, visit him at his hotel. Reporters waiting for news of the statesman were puzzled to identify the two women who were immediately taken to his room.

At the bedside Miss Cummins took up her pen and brought messages from the late President Franklin D.

Roosevelt and other of King's discarnate friends, who gave him suggestions concerning important decisions he was about to make. Other researchers who have benefited from her mediumship were the distinguished scientist Sir William Barrett; Lord Balfour, the former prime minister of Great Britain; W. B. Yeats, the Irish poet; and numerous widely known clergymen, including Drayton Thomas.

We asked Miss Cummins the method she employed to obtain her writings. She said that she sits at a table, covers her eyes with her left hand, and concentrates on "stillness." Soon she is in a condition of half-sleep, a kind of dream state, which in its own peculiar way sometimes has more illumination than one's waking state. At times she has the sensation of a dreamer who has no conscious control over the ideas that are being formulated, that she is merely a listener. "I have all the consciousness," Miss Cummins said, "that my brain is being used by a stranger all the time. It is just as if an endless telegram is being tapped out on it."

Although at the time of our visit she was working on projects of helpfulness with several people for whom she was reserving her time and strength, she herself offered to try to secure a brief communication in writing for us. She sat at the table in the living room and rested her head upon her hand for a few minutes in silence and then began to write. She wrote steadily for about fifteen minutes, one of us removing the sheet as she came to the end of each page. At the end of that time, she seemed to come to herself, as one might arouse from a sort of daydream, and read to us what she had received, crossing each "t" and dotting each "i" as she read. The writing contained a personal message for my son.

Our visit with Miss Cummins seemed to carry interesting psychic overtones. Among the wealth of Cleophas materials, there are two little booklets, *After Pentecost* and *The Resurrection of Christ*, both printed years ago in a very limited edition and long since out of print. Obviously, it would be almost impossible to locate copies of them. I was eager to obtain both booklets to supplement the others I already had in the series.

I had originally intended to inquire of Miss Cummins about them, but the issue slipped my mind and I did not do so. As we were leaving, she handed me a small package and said, "Here is a little gift I wanted you to have." Later, when I opened the package, I found she had included both of the little booklets I had so eagerly desired.

Miss Cummins passed into spirit life on August 24, 1969. Her posthumous papers were given to Ireland's archives by her executor-brother, Dr. Robert Cummins, to be made available to accredited psychic researchers throughout the world. The collection comprises 242 files and manuscripts, which include scores of original transmitted scripts, unpublished books, lectures and letters, as well as her final work, *Swan on a Black Sea*.[1] Robert Thouless describes this work as being some of the best evidence for human survival he has ever seen. This munificent gift to world research is now housed on permanent loan in the city of Cork, where a new center for archives of regional and national importance has been opened.

---

1   Geraldine Cummins, *Swan on a Black Sea: A Study in Automatic Writing: The Cummins-Willet Scripts* (London, Routledge and K. Paul, 1965).

five

The Bible and Psychic Phenomena

A news dispatch from Chicago recently described an interesting example of trance mediumship that had an important practical outcome in solving a murder case. The heading of the dispatch was "Victim's Own Voice Names Killer Suspect." It related how Mrs. Remibias Chua, while in a trance, spoke in the voice of a woman murdered months before and named the killer. In their search for the criminal, Chicago detectives had been unable to unearth a single clue as to his identity until Mrs. Chua gave them a lead through the information she received in her trance experience. On the basis of her evidence, a technician in the hospital where the victim had worked was charged with murder and eventually confessed.

There are two contrasting reactions to a story such as this involving, as it does, alleged communication with the dead. The first is the response of the antimiraculists, including the scientific establishment, who say that communication with the dead is impossible and could not be; the second, that of the antipsychics, who say that it is wrong and should not be.

Many of the first group regard psychic investigation with skepticism and disdain, as unworthy of serious consideration by intelligent people. The number in this group, however, is rapidly becoming smaller as the study of extrasensory phenomena takes its rightful place along with other accepted sciences. The second group bases its objection to metaphysical involvement on the argument that spiritism is expressly forbidden by the Scriptures and should be left strictly alone. This do-not-touch attitude is particularly characteristic of fundamentalist groups and extreme Biblical literalists who, as a rule, condemn any and all psychical experiences (unless, of course, it happens to them) as a manifestation of the devil.

In the early years of my psychic interest, a friend to whom I had lent a book on the subject returned it to me with this query, "Is there any passage in the New Testament where it is definitely stated that Jesus, or any of his disciples, ever communicated with the dead?" The question caught me off guard, and I had no immediate answer. Later, however, I recalled the Transfiguration experience of Jesus. On this occasion, we are told that during a period of intense and prolonged prayer, discarnate personalities became objectively real to Jesus and that he himself carried on high and solemn communication with the so-called dead. All three of the synoptic Gospels record the dramatic event, but let us look at the account as described in Luke 9:28-36.

> *He [Jesus] took Peter, John, and James with him and went up into the hills to pray. And while he was praying the appearance of his face changed and his clothes became dazzling white. Suddenly there were two men talking with him; these were Moses and Elijah,*

who appeared in glory and spoke of his departure, the destiny he was to fulfill in Jerusalem. Meanwhile, Peter and his companions had been in a deep sleep; but when they awoke, they saw his glory and the two men who stooped beside him. And as these were moving away from Jesus, Peter said to him, "Master, how good it is that we are here! Shall we make three shelters, one for you, one for Moses, and one for Elijah?"; but he spoke without knowing what he was saying.

The words were still on his lips, when there came a cloud which cast a shadow over them; they were afraid as they entered the cloud, and from it came a voice: "This is my Son, my Chosen; listen to him." When the voice had spoken, Jesus was seen to be alone. The disciples kept silence and at that time told nobody anything of what they had seen.

From the standpoint of paranormal interest, this passage is one of the most revealing episodes in the life of Jesus. It is a remarkable example of what is known as auric vision, or the phenomenon in which spirit entities are both seen and heard to speak. The account relates that two men in nonphysical bodies appeared to Jesus while he prayed, and the two were objectively real enough for the practical-minded Peter to suggest building shrines for them.

Not only is it stated that the two men talked with Jesus, but we are told the actual topic of their conversation: Jesus's approaching death at Jerusalem. It is plain that we are here concerned not with allegory or poetic symbolism, but with an actual event as historically real as the Crucifixion itself. If this be true, then Jesus himself carried on overt communication with the dead. One could hardly expect to obtain better authority for active communication with the spirit world than this.

From this point on, my friend's question led me to see the Bible as probably the most psychically oriented book in the world. Both Judaism and Christianity are derived from the spiritual and supernormal experiences of a few outstanding individuals. Among the great personalities of the Old Testament whose careers were based on supersensory powers and experiences was Joseph, who ascended to the position of supreme power and influence for the Hebrews because of a series of dreams he was able to interpret for the king of Egypt. The ministry of Isaiah, the most influential of the prophets, was based on the mystical and clairvoyant vision he had in the temple. The work of Moses, the supreme lawgiver of the Hebrew race, had its rise in his awesome experience at the burning bush.

What is true of the Old Testament is equally true for the New Testament. Christianity is largely based on the ethical insights and mystical experiences of Jesus and a few persons associated with him. The Transfiguration was only one of numerous events of supersensitivity that took place during the earthly ministry of Jesus. The experience of the Spirit descending on him at his baptism; his grim battle in the desert with the Prince of Darkness; the Divine Voice that spoke to him as he prayed, which some mistook for thunder; his experience of levitation in walking on the water; the many instances of his healing the sick, the lame, and the blind by his touch; and the stilling of the tempest or the withering of the fig tree by his word—all indicate how close and vital was his contact with the invisible world of spirit. Indeed, as he himself said, "You shall see heaven wide open, and God's angels ascending and descending upon the Son of Man" (John 1:51).

Next to Jesus himself, the Apostle Paul was the most influential figure of the New Testament and, like Jesus, had mediumistic powers of a high order. In fact, his Christian career began with a paranormal event that was destined to shape history. His conversation on the Damascus Road, however, was not the only transcendental experience he had. The Book of Acts describes five subsequent occasions when the Risen Lord, or some angelic visitant, came to Paul in a time of great need and gave him direction and encouragement. Throughout his entire Christian career, he was guided by psychic impressions, and crucial decisions were frequently made as a result of a trance or some spiritual vision he had experienced.

The early church was built on the fact of spirit phenomena; without it, Christianity would never have come into being. Fifty days after Easter, on the day of Pentecost, the disciples were gathered in an upper room in Jerusalem. As they waited together, we are told that suddenly there came from heaven the sound of a rushing, mighty wind that filled the house, and there appeared cloven tongues of fire that sat upon each of them, and they were filled with the Holy Spirit, and began to speak with other tongues (Acts 2:1-4). Such events in primitive Christianity were used as testimony to the faith and as a tool of Christian preaching. The marks of a true apostle were not alone the spoken word of preaching, but "the signs, and wonders, and mighty deeds" that accompanied the proclamation of the word.

In local congregations, such as at Cornish, charismatic manifestations were a frequent part of divine worship. Tertullian, one of the ancient church fathers, who died in the first half of the third century, brings this out in a vivid description of a certain woman, a member of his congregation, who had a special gift of extrasensory perception. The incident does not seem to have been at all exceptional, and it is evident that Tertullian is speaking from personal knowledge of the woman he describes.

We have now amongst us a sister whose lot it has been to be favored with sundry gifts of revelation, which she experiences in the spirit by ecstatic vision amidst the sacred rites of the Lord's day in the church; she converses with angels, and sometimes even with the Lord; she both sees and hears mysterious communications; some men's hearts she understands, and to them who are in need she distributes remedies for their maladies. . . . After the people are dismissed at the conclusions of the sacred services, she is in the regular habit of reporting to us whatever things she may have seen in vision (for all her communications are examined with the most scrupulous care, in order that their truth may be probed). . . . The apostles most assuredly foretold that there were to be "spiritual gifts" in the church.

The picture of Tertullian's church of the third century is a vignette of a much larger and more varied exhibition of esoteric gifts manifested in the churches of the first century. Paul recognized these gifts in his congregation at Corinth as manifestations of God's Spirit, and says, "One man, through the Spirit, has the gift of wise speech, while another, by the power of the same Spirit, can put deepest knowledge into words. Another, by the same Spirit, is granted faith; another, by the one Spirit, gifts of healing; and another miraculous powers; another has the gift of prophesy; and another ability to distinguish true spirits from the false, yet another has the gift of ecstatic utterances of different kinds, and another the ability to interpret it" (1 Cor. 12:8–10). In this list of spiritual powers that Paul mentions, three are normal and six are supernormal, or psychic, and all of them were exercised by Paul himself.

People who object to spirit communication on the grounds that it is unscriptural fail to recognize that what the New Testament church called "miracles" and what Paul called "gifts of the Spirit" are essentially the same set of psychic events with which modern psychic research deals. Only the names are different. When Jesus told the woman at the well of Sychar her past—that she had been married to five different husbands—she said, "Sir, I perceive that you are a prophet." Today, we would call this the gift of clairvoyance, or awareness of objective events without the use of the senses. Clairaudience refers to the direct voice reception, such as Paul experienced in his vision when he heard the voice of the man of Macedonia saying, "Come over into Macedonia and help us."

Precognition, or the knowledge of future events before they happen, has to do with experiences similar to that which the prophet Agabus displayed when he foretold the progress of Paul's journey to Rome. Telekinesis is the power of thought to affect the physical environment, as when Jesus multiplied the loaves and fishes to feed the five thousand. Apparition describes the type of dematerialized appearance Stephen experienced in his dying moments. In fact, almost every type of psychic phenomenon known today is recorded somewhere in the stories of the Old and New Testaments, including dreams, visions, trance experience, spiritual healings, psychometry, levitation, materialization, astral flights, clairvoyance, clairaudience, telepathy, and a wide range of ESP.

The Bible is a textbook of faith, and at the same time, it is a psychic source book from beginning to end. It is the failure of Biblical literalists to recognize and accept this close connection with scriptural events and modern paranormal phenomena that has given rise to the mistaken notion that the Bible condemns all intercourse with departed spirits, whether good or bad. The difficulty is rooted in a mistaken method of scriptural interpretation.

To understand properly the Scriptures at this point, it is necessary to remember just exactly what the Bible is. The word "bible" itself comes from the Greek word biblia, or library, and means not one book but a collection, or library, of books. These books were written by different writers over a period of a thousand years, under different circumstances and at separate historic periods. They are of various literary types: prose, poetry, history, gospels, allegories, myths, fables, sermon notes of the great prophets, letters of St. Paul to the churches, and other literary forms. To understand properly any particular verse or passage of Scripture, it is necessary to consider what type of literature it is, the historic period in which it was written, the person or persons speaking, and the circumstances under which they were speaking.

A second thing we need to keep in mind about the Scriptures is that they are no more of one piece ethically and spiritually than they are all of one piece in their literary forms. Many people still regard the Bible as an infallible and homogeneous document, all on the same spiritual level and every part of which is of equal value and significance. This is a mistaken interpretation.

The Scriptures are not a flat, uniform plain, but are like a great mountain range, with high peaks and low peaks and valleys in between. All Biblical passages are not of equal significance, either as history or for the life of faith. Nor are they ethically or morally all on the same level. For this reason, whether a scriptural text allows or forbids a particular practice is not, in itself, a sufficient guide in spiritual matters. These other factors must also be taken into account.

To understand the Biblical prohibitions against witch-craft and communication with the dead (or any other part of the Scripture, for that matter) it is necessary to take into account the times and the conditions under which they were promulgated. At the time the Mosaic legal code was promulgated, the religion of the Hebrews was in grave danger of compromise with and absorption by the pagan religions that surrounded them.

The prohibitions against witchcraft and familiar spirits were closely associated with the heathen practices of idolatry, temple prostitution, human sacrifice, and demon worship. The background of the times is described in 2 Kings 17:16–17: "Forsaking every commandment of the Lord their God, they made themselves molten images of cast metal, two calves, and also a sacred pole; they prostrated themselves to all the host of heaven and worshiped the Baal, and they made their sons and daughters pass through the fire [infant sacrifice]. They practiced augury and divination; they sold themselves to do what was wrong in the eyes of the Lord and so provoked his anger."

Such were the times out of which the Judeo-Christian Scriptures were produced. The ancient Jewish worship of the one God was encompassed by an ocean of dark paganism that threatened the very existence of a spiritual religion and against which the most rigid and uncompromising restrictions were necessary. In the heathen religions of that day, men let the spirits of the dead take the place of God, and for this reason, the Hebrew prohibitions against witchcraft and familiar spirits were made austere.

Persons who regard spiritualism, or the occult, as suspect frequently cite as justification for their position the Old Testament prohibition against "consorting with mediums." It would seem that if this commandment were valid and operative at the present time, then it would be equally necessary to observe Lev. 19:19, which reads, "You shall not allow two different kinds of beast [cattle] to mate together. You shall not plant your field with two kinds of seed. You shall not put on a garment woven with two kinds of yarn."

A person may regard the ban against mediums as morally binding and carrying divine sanctions, but it would never occur to that person to take seriously the Old Testament prohibition against eating pork or fish that have no scales or to observe the hundred and one other Jewish dietary and ceremonial laws expressly commanded or forbidden in the Mosaic law—for example, the command to break any vessel into which a mouse may have fallen or the law excluding the mother, after giving birth to a female baby, from entering the sanctuary for sixty-six days. These, and scores of other similar prohibitions in the Old Testament, we now simply pass over or ignore as having no moral relevance to us today.

We shall see later on in this chapter that there are dangers in psychic involvement, but they are no more serious than the dangers of extreme literalism in interpreting the Scriptures. The oft-quoted command of Exod. 22:18, "You shall not allow a witch to live," has had a tragic and heartbreaking history. Invariably, it was this text that was quoted to justify the hideous torture and execution of witches practiced in the past. Led by the noted eighteenth-century divine, Cotton Mather, a total of twenty-seven persons in New England alone were executed for witchcraft, one of whom was an eighty-year-old man who was pressed to death. Martin Luther himself, quoting this Scripture, said concerning the practice, "I would have no compassion on these witches. I would burn them all."

This command to exterminate all witches, which has usually been regarded by those who oppose occult things as a divine injunction proceeding directly from the mouth of God himself, should be set alongside other prescribed penalties for violation of the Old Testament code that would be unthinkable today. Here are a few examples, out of scores of similar ones from the sacred law of Moses, that we today do not carry out; in fact, if we did attempt to carry them out, we would face criminal charges.

"Work may be done on six days, but on the seventh day there is a sabbath of sacred rest, holy to the Lord. Whoever does work on the sabbath day must be put to death" (Exod. 31:15).

"When a man is discovered lying with a married woman, they shall both die, the woman as well as the man who lay with her" (Deut. 22:22).

"When a man has a son who is disobedient and out of control, and will not obey his father or his mother, or pay attention when they punish him, then his father and mother shall take hold of him and bring him out to the elders of the town, at the town gate. They shall say to the elders of the town, 'This son of ours is disobedient and out of control; he will not obey us, he is a wastrel and a drunkard.' Then all the men of the town shall stone him to death (Deut. 21:18-21).

"Whoever utters [blasphemes] the Name of the Lord shall be put to death" (Lev. 24:16).

It is not generally recognized, even by well-read Christians, that the Old Testament penalty for violation of each of the Ten Commandments is death. Yet such is the case. If the penalty for violating the above-prescribed laws were carried out against adultery, Sabbath-breaking, disobedient children, profanity, or any other of the Ten Commandments, the population of this and other countries would be considerably reduced in numbers and birth control would not be necessary.

The God who is from everlasting to everlasting does not change, but men's ideas of him change. It is plain that many of the early laws and religious practices of the

Hebrews represent a false or inadequate conception of the nature of God, far below the Christian revelation embodied in Jesus Christ. For this reason, the Old Testament commandment to kill either witches or disobedient children is not taken seriously as carrying divine sanction for us today.

As we have already noticed, the attitudes of most theologically conservative groups toward the paranormal is to have nothing to do with it, their reason being that the Bible forbids it. A more serious objection to extrasensory involvement, however, is that it has its dangers and pernicious aspects. This fact is recognized and accepted by all qualified researchers.

After years of extensive investigation of the psi field,[1] Mrs. Louisa Rhine, writing in the Newsletter of the American Society for Psychical Research, warns against the use of automatisms as a method of "tapping the unconscious," especially the dangers of the Ouija board and automatic writing. The very nature of these two, she feels, "makes them particularly open to misunderstanding."

Automatisms are simply mechanical devices for receiving psychic messages. Of all such mechanisms, the Ouija board is currently the one most widely in use. Its trademark name is a combination of the French *oui* and the German *ja*, both meaning "yes." It is therefore a "yes-yes" board, and many people turn to it, as men in high position may turn to a "yes man" for reassurance to hear what they want to hear. The thing is not something entirely new. The Greek philosopher and mathematician

---

1   Psi is a term used by parapsychologists to refer to the unknown factor(s) responsible for interactions between organisms and their environment that do not appear to conform to known laws of science.

Pythagoras, who lived in the sixth century B.C., described a comparable device in use in his day.

What makes the Ouija board move is still a mystery. A newspaper columnist, writing in the *Los Angeles Times*, reported that not one of three physicists working at the California Institute of Technology would "offer a scientific explanation for Ouija power." Probably the two most likely options are that the messages (1) are produced by an upswelling from the subconscious minds of the experimenters; or (2) originate from unknown discarnate entities, which is, in fact, what the communicators claim to be.

The Ouija seems to be a classic beginner's tool in the development of psychic interest and awareness. The procedure has become almost standard. It frequently begins when two or three persons, out of curiosity or merely as a lark, begin fooling around with a board. The thing begins to spell out messages, some of which are coherent and make sense. This is stage one. The next stage begins when some member of the group develops the ability to do automatic writing. Later, the gift of trance mediumship may emerge and use of the board is discontinued. The above sequence has been the usual procedure in the development of numerous highly gifted psychics, such as Betty White, for example.

Most of what comes through automatisms is nonsensical, contradictory, and quite innocuous, yet occasionally valuable communications in psychic literature have been received. An outstanding example of this is the Patience Worth material, which was received through Mrs. Pearl Curran, a comparatively uneducated St. Louis housewife. Beginning in 1913, Mrs. Curran produced (first via Ouija and later through automatic writing) a massive quantity of remarkable literary works that displayed unusual creative power and originality and unparalleled spontaneity of production. The ostensible source of the material was an entity named Patience Worth, who claimed to have lived in England three hundred years previously and who dictated her remarks in highly literate seventeenth-century English.

Mrs. Curran's work was done with extreme rapidity and covered a broad spectrum of subjects, including poems, aphorisms, literary chitchat, and no less than six novels. Her writings were hailed by some critics as superior in literary merit to any penned by contemporary authors; one academician pronounced her novel *The Sorry Tale* "the greatest story written of the life and times of Christ since the Gospels were finished."[1]

The psychic potential interest in the Ouija board and the high quality of the material derived through it, in such cases as that of Mrs. Curran and the automatic writings of Geraldine Cummins, prompted Stewart Edward White to predict that the board may be destined to take an honorable place with Sir Isaac Newton's apple, James Watt's teakettle, Benjamin Franklin's kite, and other historic playthings that have led to important achievements. Conversely, there have been many known instances where the use of such automatisms has been associated with unfortunate results.

An example of this is described by the late Robert Ashby, a personal friend of this author. At the time of his death, Ashby was director of research and education for the Spiritual Frontiers Fellowship International. This organization, begun in 1956, was founded to help restore to the churches an awareness of their psychical and mystical heritage. Members come from all denominations and in-

---

1   Pearl Curran, *The Sorry Tale: A Story of the Time of Christ* (New York: H. Holt and Company, 1917).

clude both clergy and laity.[1] Ashby related a distressing case of a woman in a large Midwestern city whose seventeen-year-old daughter, Linda, received a Ouija board as a Christmas present from a neighbor. Linda and her chum Wendy began sitting with the board. After a few days, they began to receive messages from a communicating entity who gave his name as Joe. The girls became intrigued and began a daily practice of going to Linda's room after school and spending two or three hours communicating with Joe.

The girls enjoyed Joe and thought his witty remarks very clever. Gradually his witticisms changed to off-color suggestions that tickled Linda and Wendy still further. The next stage was open sexual suggestions. The girls became disturbed and asked him to stop. At this, the messages became threatening, and the warnings included something Joe called "psychic rape" if they did not carry out his orders.

Wendy became so frightened that she gave up the sittings, but Linda felt it was more dangerous to stop than

---

1   Spiritual Frontiers Fellowship International (SFFI) was founded in 1956 in Illinois by 75 religious leaders and writers from around the U.S., "to encourage and interpret to the Churches, and receive interpretations from the Churches, the rising tide of interest in mystical, psychical, and paranormal experience," according to a flyer issued by SFFI. "My father and mother as well as my sister Ruth and I were members of this fellowship for many years," comments Lincoln Justice, author William Justice's son, "and participated in a number of their conferences. In the 1940s and 1950s, few people were open to such "far out" psychic experiences, especially within the organized church in America. It was a real blessing to finally have a group of people with whom we could share our interest in exploring the outposts of the spirit." For more information, contact: SFFI, P.O. Box 7868, Philadelphia, PA 19101; tel: 215-222-1991; fax: 215-222-8459; website: http://www.spiritualfrontiers.org.

to go on, for Joe had fiercely ordered her to continue them. Finally, things reached a climax—Joe told Linda she must stop school and stay at home with him since he and she were "soul mates from former lives." Punishment for failure to do this would be serious physical disfigurement or even her death at his hands.

By this time, Linda's mother realized that her daughter's condition was serious. Linda threw away the Ouija board but was afraid to continue her schooling because of Joe's threats. She became a recluse and began to sink deeper into a desperate mental condition. Her mother called Ashby long distance, asking him if he would help her daughter. However, later in the day she telephoned him again to say that Linda would not consent to see him because Joe had whispered that he would kill her if she did. Thus the case was closed and Ashby never learned what finally happened to Linda.

The pattern of the above case is all too common in Ouija board experiences. Whether the source is really some discarnate entity or the subconscious of the operators, the outcome is disturbing, frightening, and, occasionally, quite harmful. Canon John Pearce-Higgins, an Anglican clergyman and vice chairman of the church's Fellowship for Psychical and Spiritual Studies in Great Britain, encountered a number of instances of emotional conflict caused by the careless use of automatisms. He related the unhappy case of a woman who did automatic writing and was getting all sorts of "goody-goody" advice from it. She was in love with someone else's husband. Finally the man himself cut off his contact with her and she lost touch with him.

Presently, the messages told her that the man's wife had died and that he had gone to England. She was directed to go to England and find him. She sold her property and did as she was told, but could not find him.

Various mediums she consulted sent her off on false trails. The woman came for help to Canon Higgins, who advised her that the messages were false and to ignore them. The woman was reduced to poverty and had to be repatriated by the consul in London. When she returned home, she found that the man had never left the country and his wife was still alive.

Such unfortunate events as the two described above are extreme examples, but they are not isolated. The literature of parapsychology abounds in them. Most ventures with Ouija boards and automatic writings are more innocuous than they are harmful, but the point to remember is that they can, and sometimes do, get out of hand. There are two extremes to be avoided. One is to regard the Ouija board as merely a trivial plaything; the other is to accept everything that comes through it as factually true or as supernaturally inspired.

The proper attitude toward it, as in all other aspects of psychic phenomena, may be embodied in two important bits of advice: (1) take the board seriously: it is not a child's toy, and (2) do not take it too seriously: it is by no means a mouthpiece of infallible truth. In other words, the chances are that what comes through will be merely nonsense and quite harmless; on the other hand, the board may turn out to be injurious if it is used carelessly or with too great an emotional investment.

On an even more dangerous level than automatisms, however, are the psychic subcategories of devil worship, voodoo, witchcraft, hypnosis, and the use of LSD or other mind-awakening drugs. Interest in the occult has become a mass phenomenon. It is no longer uncommon for the police in some of our cities to pick up young people with ritual bags filled with implements for the celebration of the Black Mass, implements such as drugs, love potions, animal bones, and even human fingers.

A recent poll in a London newspaper revealed the fact that the "magical arts" are attracting young drug users and that alcoholics and drug addicts are not turning to the churches for help, but to the occult. Some 80 percent of the teenagers in and around London, it was revealed, had had some experience with potentially dangerous occult practices, including black magic, witchcraft, and Satanism. One of the workers making the survey said, "It is because the church has ceased to be supernatural. Young people want a divine supernatural power, not church frills."

One of the reasons for the widespread interest in psychism today is the fact that the churches have failed at the point of their greatest responsibility. It is obvious that many young people are turning to Oriental religions, Indian gurus, and psychedelic drugs, seeking a transcendental vision and an inner experience of God, which at one time was a part of the church's life but now is practically missing.

If the Christian church abdicates interest and responsibility in the paranormal, then it will lose its opportunity to properly instruct its people and protect them from charlatans, frauds, and apocalyptic sects that will gladly take over the instruction. The church must deal with the psychic field, or leave its people in the hands of whatever group, good or bad, that does deal with it.

If psychism has its dangers, so do other things we are thrown in with every day. The world is full of risky things. Walking on ice, riding in an automobile, flying an airplane, building and operating nuclear devices are all risky. Electricity is one of the most dangerous forces in modern life, but our industrial age is based on it. The dangers inherent in psychic exploration are no more than those encountered by men working on high-voltage lines. There are two things necessary for the safety of men who deal with high-powered currents: first, they must have an elementary knowledge of the nature of electricity and its workings; second, they themselves must be properly insulated, through the use of rubber gloves, boots, and other safety devices.

Similarly, these two things are imperative for those who would explore the extrasensory field. Such persons must understand something of the nature of the psychic forces with which they are dealing and how they function. In addition, they must be spiritually conditioned. The insulation, in this case, is purity of motive. Psychic talents may be turned to selfish advantage and become detrimental. As long as one's attitude is that of love and trust toward God, there can be no danger in communicating with the spirit world. The pure in heart and those devoid of self-interest are safe, but those who act from evil or selfish purposes can throw themselves open to spirits who act from evil or selfish purposes.

One of the functions of psychically gifted members of the Corinthian church was that of "discernment of spirits," that is, the ability to distinguish between good and evil discarnate entities. The early church fathers recognized that there were both good spirits and evil spirits, just as there are good men and evil men in the world about us; therefore, their injunction was "to try the spirits, whether they be of God."

It is important to keep in mind the distinction between psychical research and spiritualism. Psychical research is simply a critical and investigative approach to all extrasensory phenomena. Spiritualism is a religious practice based on belief that man survives death and that communication is possible between the incarnate and the discarnate. The one deals with metaphysical experiences as the object of study and scientific investigation; the other has made the study of such phenomena into a religion.

Personally, as a Christian, I am greatly interested in empirical evidence that life continues after death. This is not only a legitimate scientific objective but also the basic belief of Christianity itself. But I am not a spiritualist. Spiritualism as a religion has always seemed to me to be drab and uninviting and has its serious limitations. It has made a religion out of psychic experiences, and herein lies a grave danger to high and pure religion.

Christ deplored the fact that some of his followers were more concerned with miracles than with his spiritual teachings, more in love with his physical healings or the loaves and fishes than his Sermon on the Mount. But there is no substitute for fellowship with God. Communion is something far more important than communication, however meaningful the latter may be. To become occupied with discarnates more than with God is just as idolatrous as any other form of inordinate affection.

Although the Christian church as a whole has ignored the present expanding wave of interest in the metaphysical, a growing number of individual churchmen and laymen are becoming awake to the issue. Even the Reverend Billy Graham, who in past years has classified all psychical research as the work of the devil and would have nothing to do with it, has now changed his viewpoint and recognizes that it has value for the Christian faith.

In an interview with Lee Harrison in the September 7, 1976, issue of the *National Enquirer*, Reverend Graham indicated he had reversed his position. "I feel well-documented scientific evidence of life after death is important. Personally, the only evidence I need is the Bible; but many people need something more. Only strong scientific evidence will convince them; and, thankfully, that evidence is now being discovered."

Technically speaking, psychic phenomena may be divided into two broad categories: the contrived kind and the spontaneous kind. The first of these is the laboratory type, which sets up conditions for production or reception of the phenomenon and attempts to control all the factors that surround it. It is represented by the work being done in psychical research at a number of great universities and scientific foundations throughout the world, including Yale and Duke in America; and London, Cambridge, and Oxford in England. The second, and much larger field, is the great mass of personal extra-sensory experiences that are spontaneously happening to thousands of individuals every day as they go about their work; only a fractional part of these is being statistically studied and recorded.

Those who regard psychic research as a dangerous and forbidden field best left strictly alone are not going to be able to stop investigative work being done in university laboratories and scientific foundations, nor are they going to keep spontaneous cases of spirit manifestation from taking place. People will continue to experience visions and trances, see apparitions when dying, hear clairaudient voices, and have out-of-body experiences just as people have been doing since ancient times, whether such things are forbidden or not.

A growing body of people are beginning to realize that a psychic revolution of great significance for the future is taking place, a revolution comparable to that occurring in nuclear physics. This breakthrough definitely has both scientific and religious significance and should be intelligently studied and observed. There is an urgent current need to explain and interpret these phenomena, and the Christian churches are in the best possible position to do this.

Churchmen should recognize that a knowledge of the psychic field is of vital importance to Christianity today and can hold the key to the renewal of the churches. It can help to break the spell of mechanistic materialism, give to a skeptical generation an empirical basis for a belief in life after death, and revitalize present-day orthodoxy with a religion of spirit and power.

There are three possible approaches the Christian church can make toward the paranormal field: it can ignore it, oppose it as evil and try to hush it up, or recognize it and try to understand the facts about it. Since it is physically impossible to prevent spontaneous cases of a parapsychological nature and since it is highly unlikely that scientific laboratory investigations will be shut down throughout the world, then the alternative is to approach the phenomena as we do with other scientific developments in the world about us.

The question is not whether such things will go on happening, for they surely will, but whether they will be studied and better understood, ignored, feared, or ignorantly held in pious awe. People have a right to know the kind of universe they live in. Sanctified feeblemindedness has not been nor ever will be an asset to real religion. The thing that heals is simply the truth. As Christ said, "Ye shall know the truth, and the truth shall set you free."

six

A Host of Witnesses

As we have seen in the preceding chapter, the Bible is a primary witness to the reality of spirit agency and presence. It assumes the actuality of a world of spiritual beings, always close to and acting upon this world of flesh and blood. It is saturated with the accounts of spirit helpers, heavenly voices, and divine leadings. But the Bible is not the only witness to such things. There is the testimony of the race. Every century and country has contributed an overwhelming mass of facts that testify to the reality of the transcendental. History is replete with instances of persons who, under certain circumstances, have seemed to see beyond the ordinary limits of sense and to have beheld forms of beings who belong not to earth but to the invisible world.

A modern example of this is the recorded experience of Colonel Charles A. Lindbergh in his world-famous flight across the Atlantic in May 1927. Then a seminary student, I vividly remember the day of his crossing and how the world waited breathlessly for news of the courageous young pilot. No one knew then, and relatively few people are aware even today, that the outcome of the most spectacular solo flight in history was determined by spirit agency, which many persons still regard with complete skepticism and ridicule as mere fantasy. Yet Lindbergh himself has declared that he was not alone on his perilous journey but was accompanied by ghostly presences who gave him advice and messages from the world beyond.

The flight from New York to Paris, a distance of 3,610 miles, was one of the great adventures of modern times. Aviation at the time was much more dangerous than it is today. His plane, a single-engine monoplane of 220 horsepower with wings made of wood and fabric and with no de-icer, no lights, no heat, no radio, and no automatic pilot, weighed less than the electrical equipment of a modern airliner.

On his thirty-four-hour journey, Lindbergh encountered serious weather conditions in the mid-Atlantic in the form of fog and rain, sleet, and ice. A storm mass lay spread across his route and ice started to collect on his plane. He was forced to turn around and get back into the clear air immediately, then fly around any clouds he could not get over. Much of the time he was flying through thick fog by dead reckoning and with only primitive instruments to guide him.

In his book *The Spirit of St. Louis*, Lindbergh relates how he had been unable to sleep the night before the take-off, and at the end of twenty-one hours of flying, he had reached a state of drowsiness so heavy as to be in a semi-conscious state.[1] He was unable to read the instruments properly. They didn't seem to function as they should.

---

1   Charles Lindbergh, *The Spirit of St. Louis* (New York: Scribner, 1953).

During this period, while in a state of eye-open sleep, he relates that the fuselage behind him became filled with ghostly presences—"vaguely outlined forms, transparent, moving, riding weightless with me in the plane. . . . These phantoms speak with human voices—friendly, vapor-like shapes, without substance, able to vanish or appear at will, to pass in and out through the walls of the fuselage as though no walls were there . . . . First one and then another presses forward to my shoulder to speak above the engine's noise, and then draws back among the group behind.

"At times, voices come out of the air itself, clear yet far away . . . familiar voices, conversing and advising on my flight, discussing problems of my navigation, reassuring me, giving me messages of importance unattainable in ordinary life. . . . One or two, more prominent than the others, ride just behind my shoulder, close but never touching; communicating sometimes by voice and sometimes without the need of speaking."

On the twenty-fourth hour of his flight, Lindbergh finds himself again losing consciousness. His eyes close and he cannot keep them open. He strikes his face sharply with his hand but hardly feels the blow. Can he reach the Irish coast? The alternative is death and failure. For the first time, he doubts his ability to endure. He notices that the compass needle leans left of the lubber line. He noses the plane back into course but cannot keep it there. Sometimes it is two or three degrees off heading, sometimes ten, and sometimes close to twenty. He decides that he will do nothing except watch his compass needle. It works for a few minutes, but soon the nose is edging north again, as though a stronger mind than his is deciding its position.

In his twenty-eighth hour he comes in sight of the Irish coast. The wish to sleep has left him, as have the phantom voices, and he settles down for the last six hundred miles to Paris. When he reaches the southern tip of Ireland, he finds to his surprise that he is within three or four miles of being exactly on his route, closer than he had hoped to come in his fondest dreams before leaving America. In fact, considering all the factors involved in his overnight flight—the detour around the thunderheads, the swinging compass error, and the wind above the storm clouds that blew so fiercely on his tail—a differential of fifty to one hundred miles off this course by dead reckoning would have represented a remarkably small margin of error.

It would be difficult to dismiss this extraordinary experience of a man like Lindbergh as imagination or pure delusion. The practical aspect of it does not permit such an easy interpretation. Here is a man of the most realistic turn of mind, carrying out a concrete mission requiring the maximum in skill and mechanical accuracy, whose very life and destiny hinged on clear-cut rational decisions on his part. This man, finding himself at the end of his human resources, relinquished the operation of his machine to intangible spirit guides who brought his mission to a successful end.

What is the explanation of the event outcome? The agnostic materialist will have an explanation of the event that will doubtless satisfy him, but this does not alter the fact that since the dawn of history thousands of people have had comparable experiences of spirit entities.

One of the earlier ones of these on record is that of Socrates, who lived in the fifth century before Christ and who has often been spoken of as the Greek Christ. His two disciples, Plato and Xenophon, state that Socrates claimed to have a familiar genius, or spirit guide, who foretold events and sometimes prescribed conduct. Socrates believed this being to be other than himself because it revealed things unknown to him. In his memorable speech before the Athenians when on trial for his life, he says:

> You have heard me speak at sundry times and in divers places of an oracle or sign which comes to me, and is the divinity which Meletus ridicules in the indictment. This sign, which is a kind of voice, first began to come to me when I was a child; it always forbids but never commands me to do anything which I am going to do. . . . O my judges, . . . I should like to tell you of a wonderful circumstance. Hitherto, the divine faculty of which the internal oracle is the source has constantly been in the habit of opposing me even about trifles, if I was going to make a slip or error in any matter; and now as you see there has come to me that which may be thought, and is generally believed to be, the last and worse evil.
>
> But the oracle made no sign of opposition, either when I was leaving my house in the morning, or when I was on my way to the court, or while I was speaking, at anything which I was going to say; and yet I have often been stopped in the middle of a speech, but now in nothing I either said or did touching the matter in hand has the oracle opposed me. What do I take to be the explanation of this silence? I will tell you. It is an intimation that what has happened to me is a good, and that those of us who think that death is an evil are in error. For the customary sign would surely have opposed me had I been going to evil and not to good.

It was on the strength of the inner oracle's silence that Socrates made his final decision to refuse the unjust offer of his judges and chose to drink the hemlock instead.

Instances of spirit guides such as those who directed Lindbergh and Socrates are more numerous than many might imagine. In fact, many of the world's great owe their places in history to the influence of spirit agency. The "voices" of Joan of Arc, which were to determine the political future of France as a nation, are one example.

Another was the advice given Abraham Lincoln through the mediumship of the sensitive Nettie Colburn Maynard as to two crucial issues of his war policy: first, Lincoln was directed to issue his Emancipation Proclamation in spite of the strong opposition of members of his cabinet; second, he was instructed to visit the battlefield in person to bolster the sagging morale of the Union Army, an act that became the turning point of the Civil War. The late Sir Winston Churchill, whose influences on world history are not likely to be minimal, often had "psychic hunches" and, on at least one occasion while in South Africa, owed his life to the influence of spirit directives.

Experiences similar to those of Lindbergh and Socrates have been taking place for centuries, but only in comparatively recent years have such cases been statistically studied and scientifically observed. Dr. Elisabeth Kübler-Ross, the internationally known Swiss psychiatrist, has conducted extensive studies with several hundred terminally ill patients and has found that unusual or significant things often take place with them in the hours before death, happenings that would suggest special contact on the part of the dying with transcendental realities. When confronted by death, certain of her patients, particularly the aged ones, died with the expression of great happiness on their faces; often they appeared to be talking with some loved one who had died before them.

A striking example of this was reported by Sir William Barrett some years ago and is typical of many similar instances.

It is the case of a Dr. Wilson, a New York physician, who described the following strange experience he once had while attending a well-known operatic tenor during his dying moments.

It was about four o'clock in the morning and I noticed that his face was quite calm and his eyes clear. The poor fellow looked me in the face, and, taking my hand in both of his, he said, "You've been a good friend to me, doctor." Then something I shall never forget to my dying day happened—something utterly indescribable. While he appeared perfectly rational and sane as any man I have ever seen, the only way that I can express it is that he was transported into another world, and although I cannot satisfactorily explain the matter to myself, I am fully convinced that he had entered the golden city—for he said in a stronger voice than he had used since I had attended him, "There is mother! Why, mother, have you come here to see me? No, no, I am coming to see you. Just wait, mother, I am almost over. Wait, mother!"

On his face there was a look of inexpressible happiness, and the way he said the words impressed me as I have never been before, and I am as firmly convinced that he saw and talked to his mother as I am that I am sitting here. In order to preserve what I believed to be his conversation with his mother, and also to have a record of the strangest happening of my life, I immediately wrote down every word he said. It was one of the most beautiful deaths I have ever seen.

There are literally hundreds of such cases as the above now on record. Dr. Karlis Osis, director of the Research Division of the Parapsychology Foundation in New York City, sent out questionnaires to five thousand doctors and five thousand nurses across the United States requesting detailed information about their observances of terminally ill patients. He received 640 replies describing more than 35,000 cases, the results of which were published in a monograph under the title *Deathbed Observations by Physicians and Nurses*.[1] The survey showed that

---

1   Karlis Osis, *Deathbed Observations by Physicians and Nurses* (New York: Parapsychology Foundation, 1961).

an unexpectedly large percentage of the patients indicated awareness of spiritual presence as they were dying and often displayed emotions so elevated that they might be described as "exaltation."

Three-fourths of those who replied to the questionnaire described cases of patients, usually fully conscious and rational, who had visions or hallucinations of dead friends or relatives. In some instances, the patient manifested what is now commonly referred to as "Peak in Darien" experiences, the distinguishing mark of which is that the dying person sees a loved one or friend waiting to welcome him on the other side, a person he did not know was dead and whom he is often surprised or shocked to see.

There is a marked similarity between the clairvoyant visions of the dying and the phenomenon of angels in the Scriptures. Numerous instances of angelic beings are recorded in both the Old and New Testaments. In some cases, they appear to have an objective existence, while in others it is clear they are more intangible and visionary in nature. This second alternative was true for the case of Joseph, to whom Mary was betrothed. We are told that the angel of the Lord "appeared to Joseph in a dream." Since the Greek word for angel (angelikos) means "messenger," this would suggest a mental impression or flash of insight as readily as an objective visitor.

Many people who profess to believe in the reality of angels because they have read about them in the Bible actually do not take such things seriously. Billy Graham has written a book called *Angels: God's Secret Agents*,[1] but frankly admits that he has never seen one and the reason

---

1   Billy Graham, *Angels: God's Secret Agents* (Garden City, N.Y.: Doubleday, 1975).

he believes they exist is that the Bible says so. In this scientifically conditioned age, most persons would feel the need of more convincing evidence than this.

During the greater part of my adult life, I have found it difficult to regard angels as actual personalized entities. Like most people today, I have been inclined to think of them, along with Santa Claus and fairy tales, as simply poetic myth or romanticized fancy. After all, most of us have never seen an actual angel, nor do we know anyone else who has. All we have to go on is Biblical hearsay that remains beautiful but unconvincing. It was not until a few years ago, when the late Dr. S. Ralph Harlow spent a weekend in our home and gave a lecture in our church on "Evidence for Immortality from Psychic Research," that I first began to regard the angel stories in the Bible as serious historic possibilities.

Dr. Harlow was a widely known Congregational minister, who, at the time of his visit, was professor emeritus of Biblical language and literature at Smith College in Northampton, Massachusetts, where he had taught for thirty years. The amazing experience he related in his lecture and that was published in his valuable book *A Life after Death*, took place during the midterm vacation of his college while he and his wife, Marion, were walking through a wood near Ballardville on a lovely May morning.[1]

As they strolled hand in hand near a brook, they heard the murmur of muted voices in the distance, which they took to be a party of picnickers. The voices were coming nearer, and at a faster pace than they were walking, so they realized that the strangers would soon overtake them. Then they suddenly became aware that the sounds

---

1   Samuel Ralph Harlow and Evan Hill, *A Life after Death* (New York: Doubleday, 1961).

were not only behind them but also above them, and they looked up.

"How can I describe what we felt?" said Dr. Harlow. "Is it possible to tell of the surge of exaltation that ran through us? Is it possible to record this phenomenon in objective accuracy and yet be credible?

"For about ten feet above us, and slightly to our left, was a floating group of spirits—of angels—of glorious, beautiful creatures that glowed with spiritual beauty. We stopped and stared as they passed above us. "There were six of them, young beautiful women dressed in flowing white garments and engaged in earnest conversation. If they were aware of our existence, they gave no indication of it. Their faces were perfectly clear to us, and one woman, slightly older than the rest, was especially beautiful. Her dark hair was pulled back in what today we would call a ponytail, and although I cannot say it was bound at the back of her head, it appeared to be. She was talking intently to a younger spirit whose back was toward us and who looked up into the face of the woman who was talking.

"Neither Marion nor I could understand their words although their voices were clearly heard. The sound was somewhat like hearing but being unable to understand a group of people talking outside a house with all the windows and doors shut.

"They seemed to float past us, and their graceful motions seemed natural—as gentle and peaceful as the morning itself. As they passed, their conversation grew fainter and fainter until it faded out entirely, and we stood transfixed on the spot, still holding hands and still with the vision before our eyes."

To say that the Harlows were astonished would be an understatement. They looked at each other in amazement, each wondering if the other had also seen. Finally, to test the accuracy of his own eyes and ears to see if he had been the victim of hallucination or imagination, Harlow led his wife to a fallen birch and said, "Now, Marion, what did you see? Tell me exactly, in precise detail. And tell me what you heard." Her reply was identical in every respect to what his own senses had reported. "It seems to me," she said as she finished, "that for those split seconds the veil between our world and the spirit world was lifted and for some reason, unknown to us, we were permitted to see and hear what generally our physical eyes and ears are unable to sense."

Harlow went on to say that the experience had greatly altered his thinking about the Nativity and Resurrection stories of the New Testament. For years, he had wondered if these accounts had been accurately reported, or if they were simply legend based on fantasy. As a child he had accepted angels as literal heavenly personages, but as a mature man, he came to regard them as symbolic or poetic images injected into stories of the imagination. Now, since his encounter with the six angels, his skepticism has left him and he accepts the fact that back of the Christmas story, as recorded by Luke, may well be a genuine, objective experience in which angel visitors were seen and heard by human eyes and ears. However, he said he could not be dogmatic at this point, as is the fundamentalist in his strong belief or the materialistic psychologist who is equally dogmatic in his denial of it.

Some months after this, the Harlows were attending a conference of Sunday School leaders and teachers at the University of New Hampshire. At the lunch hour, with several ministers present, the conversation turned to the question of immortality, which had been discussed in some of the classes that morning, and Marion related their Ballardville experience with the angels. The luncheon group listened, at first with eager interest, and then with strained politeness. Finally one minister, unable to conceal his contempt, snorted, "It must have been a flock of bees!"

Up to the time when I first heard Harlow relate his Ballardville encounter with angels, I had never heard of a similar experience in the entire literature of psychism and did not imagine that, even supernormally, such things ever took place in real life. Since then, however, I have come to know other rare individuals who have had comparable experiences. One such person, a dear friend of lofty character and deep personal commitment, has told us that she herself, in certain exceptionable moments, has experienced angelic beings visible to the eye. On one such occasion, as she and a friend were returning from a retreat in the Rocky Mountains, she saw a company of angels near the highway on which they were driving. Here is her description of her beautiful vision.

Our prayer group used to go to a little cabin in the mountains for special prayer for the world. Once when we had been there two days, my prayer partner and I were driving home. Suddenly as we drove past a lovely valley on the right, I became conscious that there were angels in the valley near the highway, a great host of them. It surprised me that I should see angels in such mundane circumstances as that of driving along the highway.

At first, I simply had a feeling that something was out there, but all of a sudden, I saw clearly their shape and form and color. They filled the little valley and were floating and swooping in circular motions near the earth. I saw their faces. They were beautiful—masculine and feminine, both—I could not always tell the difference. Their bodies and clothing seemed to be all of one piece and there was great joy in all their colors and movements. The intensity of their focus of blessing was something that was indescribable. We could not stop on the highway because of the traffic situation. Although we had to go on, we did not regret having to leave because we felt that the blessing had come and that it was it.

On another occasion while attending a retreat, I was out walking in the early evening. The moon had just risen. It was a special time of high communion and I was very much aware of the presence of God. Suddenly, it seemed He said to me, "Open your eyes." Then to my great astonishment, I saw four angels of tremendous size. They seemed to be of the stature of earth to heaven. The first time I saw them they were all together. There was great solemnity in their countenances, and they seemed to be in some sort of conference. I saw them only briefly, but I seemed to know that they were special heavenly workers on behalf of our planet.

The second time I saw them I was on a hilltop, and they came from four different directions. Their clothing was gorgeous in color, more intense than the angels I saw in the mountain valley. The one from the north was blue, from the east yellow, from the west red, and from the south green. Again, they were of wondrous height, and again, there was solemnity and a great sense of a meeting of heavenly personages.

The knowledge deepened in me in that these angels were on special assignment to our earth, to help save our earth. I shared my experience with our prayer group at the retreat, and this not only made us more conscious of our need to pray for the world but also gave us new hope for the world as we continued to be aware of our heavenly helpers. Later, I saw them several times—always in isolated areas.

These unheard-of experiences of two of our close friends, whose judgment and integrity it is impossible to doubt, put the reality of angels, for me, on a more credible basis. Seeing angels is no everyday occurrence, no more than is hearing heavenly music. Yet the two are inextricably linked in the Christmas story. The angel who appeared to the shepherds in the fields of Bethlehem was accompanied by a multitude of the heavenly host, "praising God and saying, 'Glory to God in the highest.'" Other friends have told us that, on certain occasions, the inaudible has become audible and they themselves have heard such music.

One such case is that of Alice Ward, the wife of my friend Dr. Dudley Ward, formerly secretary of the Board of Church and Society of the United Methodist Church in Washington, D.C., I never had the privilege of knowing Alice, who died a few years ago after a long bout with cancer. But those who knew her intimately spoke of her in the highest terms as an angelic being of unusual spiritual powers and of an exceptionally profound prayer life.

On one occasion, while praying for a friend who was undergoing a serious operation in the hospital, she heard a celestial choir singing and had the strong assurance given her that the surgery then taking place would be successful. "As I entered into the silence," she wrote in her valuable little book, *Servant of the Light*,[1] "I became aware of joy and freedom surging through my entire being. Then I heard music and listened as the music came closer to me and increased in its beauty. Gradually this music, sung by a heavenly choir, enveloped me."

During her friend's recovery, each time Mrs. Ward sat in the silence of her prayer period, she could hear the music. Later, she gave herself "completely for the use of the Spirit" on behalf of a male friend of Germanic background who was undergoing surgery. Again she became aware of music from a distance but could not discern

---

1   Alice Armstrong Ward with A. Dudley Ward, *Servant of Light* (Nashville, Tenn.: Tidings, 1972).

either the words or tune. After a time, it moved closer and enveloped her. It seemed as if all the choirs of heaven were singing.

This time the music was not in English but in a foreign tongue. Again and again it would come to her in her periods of silence, always in the same language she had heard initially. Later, she heard the music sung in English by a church choir and was able to identify it as the German music she had been hearing.

One of the most striking and exceptional cases on record of hearing supernatural music is that related by Bayard Taylor. Taylor, a nineteenth-century American poet who served for a number of years as United States ambassador to Germany, heard an invisible choir break out in an exalted song one night while he was camping in the Yosemite Valley. He described his incredible experience in an article in the *New York Mercury*:

> *It was, perhaps, an hour past midnight, along the foothills of the Nevadas, when, as I lay with open eyes gazing into the eternal beauty of night, I was conscious of a deep, murmuring sound, like that of a rising wind. I looked at the trees; every branch was unmoved—yet the sound was increased, until the air of the lonely dell seemed to vibrate with its burden. A strange feeling of awe and expectancy took possession of me. Not a dead leaf stirred on the boughs; while the mighty sound—a choral hymn, sung by ten thousand voices—swept down over the hills, and rolled away like retreating thunder over the plain.*
>
> *It was no longer the roar of the wind. As in the wandering prelude of an organ melody, note trod upon note with slow, majestic footsteps, until they gathered to a theme, and then came the words, simultaneously chanted by an immeasurable host: 'Vivant terrestriae!' The air was filled with the tremendous sound, which seemed to sweep near the surface of the earth, in powerful waves, without echo or reverberation.*

Suddenly, far overhead, in the depths of the sky, rang a single clear, piercing voice of unnatural sweetness. Beyond the reach of human organs, or any human instrument, its keen alto pierced the firmament like a straight white line of electric fire. As it shot downward, gathering in force, the vast terrestrial chorus gradually dispersed into silence, and only that one unearthly sound remained. It vibrated slowly into the fragment of a melody, unlike any which had ever reached my ears—a long undulating cry of victory and joy; while the words 'Vivat Coelum!' were repeated more and more faintly, as the voices slowly withdrew, like a fading beam of sunset, into the abysses of the stars. Then all was silent.

I was undeniably awake at the time and could recall neither fact, reflection, nor fancy of a nature to suggest the sounds. . . . How does faculty of the brain act, so far beyond our conscious knowledge, as to astound us with the most unexpected images? Why should it speak in the Latin tongue? How did it compose music—which would be as impossible for me as to write a Sanskrit poem?

There are striking similarities between this unique experience of Bayard Taylor and the Bethlehem event. Both took place at night and in the outdoors, under the open sky. Both were audible to human ears and seemingly came from some distance away. Although we are not told in what language the host of Bethlehem sang, it must have been in Hebrew or Aramaic if the shepherds were to understand it. Oddly enough, the Yosemite choir sang in Latin, which, with Taylor's cultural background, was sufficient for him to catch the general import of its words.

As we have already noticed, there are many things in the Bible that have their modern counterparts. If we accept the New Testament account of an angelic host singing the "Gloria in Excelsis Deo" as an historical event, there is no logical reason for rejecting Taylor's description of a supernatural choir singing at midnight. If such a thing could happen once, there is nothing to prevent its happening again.

One of the puzzling aspects of Taylor's experience is its intent. Why did a supernatural company of spirits become vocal to a solitary individual? One can justify the visit of the heavenly host to the shepherds of Bethlehem as part of the total celebration of the greatest event in human history. Also, one can explain the spirit presences that assisted Lindbergh on his transatlantic journey as being necessary for the preservation of his life and the accomplishment of his important mission. But why should a spirit host sing to Bayard Taylor in the dead of night, for no apparent reason in the world, or why did six angels become visible to Ralph and Marion Harlow as they strolled in broad daylight through the Ballardville woods? Wonderful and mysterious indeed is this universe in which we live.

seven

The Verdict of the Experimentalists

In the preceding chapters we have seen how the Bible bears witness to the validity of spirit phenomena and guidance, and that the testimony that such things do take place is equally overwhelming. In this chapter we shall take up the testimony of the experimentalists, the hard-core evidence of men of science who have made extensive explorations in the paranormal field.

As we have already noticed, when Dr. J. B. Rhine began his pioneer work in extrasensory perception in the 1930s, he began it as an exploration of the inner consciousness. The experimental work that has since been done in this area has been largely a study of the mind and its powers. While some parapsychologists have attempted to demonstrate the fact of human survival of death, most of the laboratory scientists are interested in the subject from a scientific, not a religious, motive. By literally thousands of experiments, conducted under rigid laboratory conditions, Dr. Rhine himself and his associates have produced well-nigh unimpeachable evidence for the reality of three amazing truths:

1. Telepathy is a fact. Mind can influence mind without the aid of the physical senses.
2. Precognition is a fact. The mind has the power of projecting itself into the future and knowing certain things in advance.
3. Psychokinesis—"the measurable force of the mind"—is a fact. Mind cannot only affect other minds, but it can affect the movement of physical objects as well, in a way that can be demonstrated and measured.

At the time of our visit with Dr. Rhine, we were particularly interested in observing the dice-throwing machine used in his laboratory for psychokinetic tests. A person standing by this mechanically operated device, wishing for certain results, could affect the roll of the dice. We were told that hundreds of tests over several years resulted in mathematical statistics showing that the desired number appeared more often than other figures dictated by chance. Some outside force, while slight, was unmistakably at work. The odds against obtaining these results by mere chance require a number twenty digits long.

The movement of physical objects without visible cause goes counter to ordinary experience and contradicts common sense. Such things just could not happen. Yet the evidence is overwhelming that such things do take place. Capable scientists throughout the world are investigating the physical aspects of the paranormal and are coming up with results that are authentic and startling.

In demonstrating the nonphysical properties of the human mind, Dr. Rhine felt that he had made a major contribution toward proving the fact of the immortality of the soul. He recognized, however, that the actuality of telepathy and psychokinesis cannot in itself prove that human personality goes on living after death. What that actuality does is give scientific support of a spiritual order, and that in itself, he held, is a great gain in establishing scientific evidence for immortality.

Sir William Crookes, the distinguished British physicist whose discovery and bending of the cathode ray laid the foundations of electronics and prepared the way for nuclear fission, was the first leading man of science who experimentally explored the physical type of psychic phenomena. He began his inquiry into the subject believing that such things were simply superstition and trickery, but he ended up by staking his scientific reputation on the fact that his preconceived ideas were wrong and that a class of phenomena, wholly new to science, did really exist.

Crookes was elected president of the prestigious Royal Academy of Science but was later dropped because he refused to give up his investigative work in psychic research. Some of the lesser scientists doubtless felt they would be stigmatized by his interests if he were permitted to continue his work unpenalized. Ten years later, however, he was reelected president of the academy because he was unquestionably Britain's greatest scientist at that time.

During his investigative work with the noted sensitive D. D. Home and others extending over a period of years, Crookes carried out hundreds of experiments in his home under strict test conditions. He summed up the result of his research into materializations, ectoplasm, levitations, and other psychic forces by saying, "I have both seen and heard, in a manner which would make unbelief impossible, things called spiritual, which cannot be taken by a rational being to be capable of explanation by imposture, coincidence, or mistake. I do not say these things are possible. I say that they exist."

Among the physical types of mediumship Crookes observed in hundreds of experiments he conducted in the presence of trusted witnesses, in his home and in daylight, were the following:

1. The movement of heavy bodies, such as tables, chairs, and sofas, without contact with any person.
2. The alteration of the weight of bodies. A balance apparatus, specially constructed for the test, revealed that the force of gravity would often fluctuate, and objects weighing from ten to twenty-five pounds, under the influence of the psychic force, would become so heavy that it was difficult for persons to lift the weight.
3. The levitation of human beings. A person sitting on a chair might be levitated several inches, or feet from the floor, remain suspended for a short period, and then descend to the floor.
4. The playing of tunes on musical instruments (usually an accordion for convenience or portability) without direct human intervention, under conditions rendering contact or communication with the keys impossible. Often the accordion floated about in the wire cage prepared for the testing and continued to play, with no person touching it and no hand being near it.

Crookes summed up his report to the Quarterly Journal of Science by saying: "It will be seen that the facts are of the most astounding character, and are seen utterly irreconcilable with all the known theories of modern science.... That certain psychical phenomena, such as the movement of material substances, and the production of sounds resembling electric discharges, occur under circumstances in which they cannot be explained by any physical law at present known is a fact of which I am as certain as I am of the most elementary fact in chemistry....The facts point to another order of life continuous with this, and demonstrate the possibility, in certain circumstances of communication, between this world and the next."

Although Crookes was the first great physical scientist to test metaphysical realities by modern experimental techniques, he was followed shortly thereafter by a number of scientists of the highest order, such as Britain's great physicist Sir Oliver Lodge; Dr. Hans Driesch, professor of philosophy at Leipzig; Italy's noted psychiatrist and criminologist Cesare Lombroso; Professor and Madame Curie, the discoverers of radium; and the outstanding French astronomer Camille Flammarion, a member of the French Academy of Science, who investigated psychic phenomena for more than sixty years and produced ten books on the subject.

All of these persons conducted extensive studies in the paranormal field and reached strikingly similar conclusions as to the reality of what they found. The work of Charles Richet, professor of psychology at the University of Paris, a Nobel Prize winner, and author of *Thirty Years of Psychical Research*, suggests the scope and nature of the results attained by the entire group.[1] Richet sums up the results of more than three decades of personal investigation of the paranormal by declaring that the following startling truths "have been placed beyond doubt":

1. The reality of cryptesthesia (the human mind has sources of cognition that disclose facts that neither sight, hearing, nor touch could reveal); and
2. The reality of ectoplasms or materializations (there are powers emerging from the human body that can take form and act as if they were material bodies).

---

1   Charles Richet, *Thirty Years of Pyschical Research* (New York: Arno Press, 1975).

Concerning the latter he writes:

I shall not waste time in stating the absurdities, almost the impossibilities, from a psychophysiological point of view, of this phenomenon. A living being, or living matter, formed under our eyes which has its proper warmth, apparently a circulation of blood, and a physiological respiration . . . which has also a kind of psychic personality having a will distinct from the medium, in a word, a new human being! This is surely the climax of marvels! Nevertheless, it is a fact.

I say that under certain exceptional conditions—and I admit that these conditions are extremely exceptional—the semblance of a living hand is formed which has all the properties of a living hand and seems to belong to a being similar to a human being!

I am firmly convinced that there are real physical metaphysical phenomena.

On one of the travel seminars my wife and I conducted to the Soviet Union, we were privileged to visit Victor Adamenko, a well-known Russian physicist, in Moscow. Although a physicist by vocation, Dr. Adamenko was deeply involved in the paranormal field and had done extensive research in psychokinesis and the Kirlian photography. We knew of him and his work by reading *Psychic Discoveries behind the Iron Curtain*, a book written by Sheila Ostrander and Lynn Schroeder, two young American women who had traveled for two years in the Soviet Union, Bulgaria, and Czechoslovakia, interviewing top scientists and exploring the facts behind psychic research in the laboratories of those countries.[1]

For an hour we chatted with Dr. Adamenko in our hotel room about things paranormal. He told us that the

---

1   Sheila Ostrander and Lynn Schroeder, *Psychic Discoveries behind the Iron Curtain* (Englewood Cliffs, N.J.: Prentice-Hall, 1970).

Soviet scientists are vitally interested in the field and knew a lot about ESP research outside their own country. They know all about Edgar Cayce, "the sleeping prophet," and had even had a lecture on him in Moscow. They are interested in Gerard Croiset, the Dutch psychic famous for his work with police in solving crimes, and are deeply fascinated with the American, Ted Serios, who reputedly is able to make photographs of distant objects appear on a film by merely staring at the camera. "Russian parapsychologists," he said, "are no longer trying to prove that ESP exists. They are now trying to find out how and why psi works."

Adamenko described the outcome of some of his work with psychokinesis and presented us with written copies of tests he had conducted demonstrating the fact that objects could be moved at a distance by means of controlled bioelectrical fields. In fact, he told us that his wife, Alla Vinogradove, a professor of psychology, was highly mediumistic and, on occasions, had participated in filmed demonstrations of psychokinetic ability in Moscow.

At such times, she performed feats of mind over matter, such as causing needles, fountain pens, and other small objects to move by the energy of thought alone. During such tests, while holding her hand six inches above an aluminum cigar case, the object would move across a plexiglass table until she stopped it. It was also shown that though motion of an arm over two targets placed close to each other was identical, only that target on which the subject's attention was concentrated started moving.

One of the most mysterious and baffling aspects of the psi field is that of the poltergeist phenomenon. The term poltergeist is derived from the German word for mischievous ghost, suggested by the fact that objects are often disturbed in a prankish way. In certain locations around the world, especially in certain houses, mysterious knocks or explosive sounds, flying stones, the breaking of crockery or glassware, and the moving and overturning of furniture have been reported for many years.

Exactly what causes these manifestations is still a mystery. The phenomena often seem to center around a young person between the ages of ten and twenty. In fact, when a parapsychologist is confronted by a case of poltergeist activity, his first question will probably be, "Is there an adolescent in the house?" Nearly always the answer is yes. Very often the adolescent boy or girl is at the period of puberty and may be undergoing some hidden, severe emotional problems. It would seem that the turmoil of the inner mental state of the young person may be transmuted into some kind of energy capable of moving physical objects in his vicinity. Often the focus person is unaware of his part in the disturbances.

A classic example of poltergeist activity is the haunting of the Epworth rectory, the childhood home of John Wesley, founder of Methodism. During the winter of 1717, the rectory at Epworth, England, became the scene of numerous psychic manifestations that continued for several months. During this time, the occupants of the house would hear strange noises throughout the day or night. Soon the Wesleys began to refer to the ghost as Old Jeffrey. Jeffrey's behavior occupied the major attention of the family for a considerable time. Often they were so perturbed that they would sit up until one or two o'clock, listening to the knocking, which might go on for hours.

On one occasion, one of the girls was on the garret stairs when Old Jeffrey's footsteps were heard coming down. He passed her and, though he was invisible, each step he took actually shook the stairs. Once Mrs. Wesley heard a knocking on the door and rushed to open it. Finding no one there, she tried to shut the door, but it was pushed against her so vigorously that she had great difficulty closing and latching it. The rector himself was several times given a push by the invisible being when he went to enter his study. When the manifestation began, the family watchdog would cringe in abject terror.

One of Old Jeffrey's antics greatly annoyed the rector, John Wesley's father, Samuel. The Wesleys were made to realize that the ghost greatly disliked the prince of Orange and the House of Hanover. At family prayers when Mr. Wesley prayed for King George and the prince, Jeffrey would interrupt with loud rappings. It was evident that he was either a radical republican or a Jacobite, for he certainly did not show proper respect for the royal family. After several months of these strange happenings, the Wesleys made up their minds to move out of the haunted rectory, but before they had completed all arrangements, the disturbances suddenly ended and were never heard again.

Among numerous modern examples of poltergeist phenomena is the case of Matthew Manning, an authentic young English psychic around whom amazing and unexplainable things frequently take place. The events that occur in Manning's home have characteristics common to most poltergeist cases, and a lot besides. A shower of pebbles may fall from the ceiling; objects are seen to rise several feet from the floor, hang in the air, and then slowly float down to the floor again; doors are closed and locked but minutes later are found opened. Objects frequently are moved about with no apparent reason. It is not unusual to find the kettle in the refrigerator, all of the chairs placed on the table, a hat hung on a nail where a picture has been, or a broom balanced across the back of a chair.

These things not only take place within the home; they sometimes take place outside as well. At times Manning's presence seems to have a most peculiar effect on the car in which he is traveling. On several journeys he made, the engine would cut out for no visible reason, as if the ignition had been switched off. While driving along at a speed of sixty miles an hour, the car would come to a halt and refuse to start again. The remedy found after some experience with this was for Manning to get out of the car, after which the engine would start immediately.

So extraordinary are Manning's paranormal gifts that Dr. George Owen, director of the New Horizon Research Foundation in Toronto and formerly a professor at Cambridge University, England, convened a seminar in June 1974. Twenty-one leading scientists from the Western world were invited to carry out tests of Manning's psychokinetic abilities. Experiments were carried out with Matthew Manning during the three weeks of the Toronto conference.

Among the men of science who participated in the experiments was Professor Brian Josephson, widely recognized physicist and a Nobel Prize recipient. Following the conference, Professor Josephson, in a press interview, said: "We are on the verge of discoveries which may be extremely important for physics. We are dealing here with a new kind of energy. This force must be subject to laws. I believe ordinary methods of scientific investigation will tell us much about psychic phenomena. They are mysterious, but they are no more mysterious than a lot of other things in physics already. In times past, 'respectable' scientists would have nothing to do with psychical phenomena; many of them still won't. I think that the 'respectable' scientists may find they have missed the boat."

Probably the most extensive work now being done in the poltergeist area is being done in Germany under the direction of Professor Hans Bender, director of the Institute of Psychology of the University of Freiburg. Dr. Bender, who has established a reputation as Germany's foremost parapsychologist, began his work right after World War II. Since that time, he has conducted intensive studies of hundreds of paranormal cases coming under his notice, including that of apports, or the passage of one object through the supposedly impenetrable matter of another.

One of a number of such apports reported by him occurred in the home of the mayor of Neudorf, a village of Baden, where four persons witnessed showers of iron nails falling from the ceiling of one of the mayor's rooms sixteen times in forty-five minutes. The origin of the nails was later traced to a locked cupboard in the basement.

Some objects, instead of falling, were seen to move upward. The mayor himself saw a clothespin climb straight up to the top of a door and then continue to fly at a right angle. Other witnesses independently described how they saw objects rush out of a wall. "Thus," Dr. Bender comments, "I was once more confronted with the apparent phenomena of teleportation and the penetration of matter through matter."

There are striking similarities between the poltergeist phenomenon and the much-talked-about unidentified flying objects, now commonly spoken of as UFOs. Both have a way of appearing and disappearing as if by magic. Sometimes they make audible sounds and at other times their movement is silent. Both seem to be under the direction of an active intelligence.

It has been generally assumed that these unknown flying objects, if they really exist, are spaceships from some nearby planet. However, certain reputable scientists seriously consider the possibility that UFOs are not necessarily extraterrestrial visitors but may be paraphysical in nature and exist in another dimension or "frequency" unrestricted by spatial limitations. Dr. J. Allen Hynek, the man who from firsthand, personal investigation knows more about the subject than any other, now leans strongly toward this view. If this concept of coexisting worlds, or a multifrequency universe, should prove to be correct, then it could easily turn out that the explanation for UFOs would be nearer to the field of parapsychology than to that of astronomy.

One of the latest and most challenging developments in psychical research is that of the electronic voice phenomenon. Strange, unaccountable voices purporting to be those of deceased persons are mysteriously appearing on electromagnetic tape. The event has created an entirely new situation in the realm of parapsychological research. Dr. Bender himself feels that the voice phenomenon may turn out to be as important, if not more so, than the discovery of nuclear physics.

In some way, and for reasons still not understood, voices of dead persons linked with the experimenter by affection or interest appear during playbacks of tape recordings on which no such voices were audible at the time of the original recording. The tape voices appear without human intervention and are inaudible to persons present during the recording, presenting an enigma to the physical scientists that so far has remained unsolved.

Since the microphone is the electronic image of the human ear and is only able to pick up what is audible to it, how can the microphone hear something that the human ear cannot? The average microphone can pick up sound waves with a range of from 60 cycles per second (the very low sounds) to 12,000 cycles per second (very high sounds). This corresponds approximately to the average range of the human ear, which is unable to register sounds outside this range. If there are voices or noises on the tape, then all the people in the room during the recording should be able to hear them while they are being recorded. However, this is not the case.

Not only are the electronic aspects puzzling, there are linguistic problems as well, such as the content and nature of the speech itself. The voices from the beyond come across at double the speed of our own speech and at a frequency that is difficult for the human ear to adjust to. The sentences have an unmistakable rhythm and are clipped and abbreviated as in a telegram. In addition, the voice entities speak in a mixture of languages, sometimes as many as three or four in one sentence.

Electronic voices were discovered in 1959 by Friedrich Jürgenson, a Swedish author and film producer living at Mölnbo, Sweden. On one occasion, Jürgenson was attempting to record the song of the Swedish finch for a movie he was making. Something seemed to go wrong with his equipment and he was perplexed to hear extraneous sounds on the recordings. Thinking that perhaps the recorder had developed a fault, he took it for an overhaul, but nothing could be found wrong with it. Later, he became convinced that the mix-up was something more than coincidence.

Jürgenson says: "A few weeks later I went to a small forest hut near Stockholm and attempted another experiment. I did, of course, have no idea what I was looking for. I put the microphone in the window. The recording I made passed without incident. On playback, I first heard some twittering of birds in the distance, then silence. Suddenly, from nowhere came a voice, a woman's voice in German: 'Freidel, my little Freidel, can you hear me?' It was as if the speaker had to make a tremendous effort to speak and the voice sounded anxious. But I am sure beyond a shadow of a doubt that this was the unmistakable voice of my mother who called me by name. My mother had died four years earlier in Sweden. That was how it began. "

An interesting aspect of Jürgenson's discovery was that it was not something that happened by accident or pure chance; instead, he seemed to have had instructions or intuition from another dimension. An unexplainable urge moved him to experiment. He says, "I find it extremely difficult to describe exactly why I carried out these experiments; somehow, and completely without any known reason, there grew in me an overwhelming desire to establish electronic contact with something or somebody unknown. It was a strange feeling; almost as if I had to open a channel for something which was still hidden and wanted to get into the open. "

From this point on, Jürgenson set out deliberately to record and study the voices. He took samples of his tapes to the Central Office for Telegraphic Technology in Berlin, where visual voice prints proved that the taped voices had all the characteristics of the human voice. After four years of systematic and intensive experimentation, he decided that the evidence and its implications were too important not to be shared with others, so he called an international press conference at which he played his tapes and made known his feelings. Following this, he published a report of his experiments in Swedish, called *Rosterna fran Rydem* (*Voices from Space*).

As a result of reading this account, Dr. Konstantin Raudive, a Latvian psychologist living in southern Germany, visited Jürgenson in his Swedish laboratory. The two made numerous successful recordings together and continued their joint efforts for some time. Later, Dr. Raudive continued his experiments independently. In 1968 he published the results of his work in German in a book called *Unhörbares Wird Höbar* (The Inaudible Becomes Audible). The book was later translated and published in England under the title *Breakthrough*.[1] It contained detailed accounts of voices recorded and analyzed by Raudive, with a preface written by Peter Bander, the joint partner with Colin Smythe in the publishing firm of Colin Smythe Ltd., which published it.

The translation and publication of the book in English proved to be an interesting and significant story in itself. Colin Smythe, attending the Frankfurt Book Fair in October 1969, met Dr. Raudive, who gave him a copy of the book. He brought it back to his colleague Peter Bander for him to evaluate and advise whether it might be published in English translation. The contents of the book were so amazing that at first Bander was inclined to advise against its publication. But in the meantime, unknown to him, Colin Smythe had purchased a number of recording tapes and, following the written instructions in Dr. Raudive's books as to the method to be used, he had proceeded to make an experiment on his own, an experiment that changed Bander's mind.

Smythe's first attempt at recordings had yielded a clearly audible voice with a certain peculiar rhythm, but he was unable to make sense out of it. He left it on the recording machine for Bander, who later listened to alone in his office. At first Bander heard nothing. He played it back five times and was just about to give up when he heard its rhythm. He played it once more and suddenly he heard a voice, quite distant but very clear. He replayed the tape, for he was afraid he had fallen victim to his own imagination. This time the voice came in even clearer. It was a woman's voice that said in German, "*Mach die Tur mal auf.* Why don't you open the door?"

---

1   Published in English as Konstantin Raudive, *Breakthrough: An Amazing Experiment in Electronic Communication with the Dead* (Garrauds Cross, U.K.: Smythe, 1971).

Two days before, an incident had taken place that gave point to the whole experiment. The office staff had reproached Bander because he had been keeping his office door closed. Although Bander had been accustomed to keeping his office door closed while working, apparently his colleagues and friends had found him completely unapproachable and told him so.

Bander comments: "This in itself might not appear significant to an outsider . . . but for two facts. As soon as I heard the voice, I recognized the speaker; although the voice spoke terribly fast and in a strange rhythm, I had heard it many times before. For eleven years before her death, I had conducted my entire correspondence with my mother by tape, and I would recognize her voice anywhere. And this was my mother's voice. Secondly, Colin Smythe cannot speak German and in any event is quite incapable of playing a deceitful trick of this kind on anybody."

Because of the startling nature of its contents, it was decided that the publication of *Breakthrough* would depend on the nature of careful tests by British electronics experts. Dr. Raudive was invited to England to demonstrate his tapes in the presence of competent witnesses who would examine every single item used during the recordings. The group was made up of twenty persons, including a number of highly respected members of the academic world, an electrical engineer, a high dignitary of the Roman Catholic Church, and two experts in electronics. As the group listened, a number of voice entities were heard. All group members agreed, at the end of the session, that the voices were there and by all the laws of physics should not have been there.

Shortly after *Breakthrough* came off the press, my wife and I had the opportunity of spending an evening with Peter Bander and Colin Smythe in Garrauds on the outskirts of London. Richard Sheargold, an engineer who has become one of Britain's leading amateur researchers in the field of paranormal voices, was also present with his wife as guests of Bander. We spent an interesting evening discussing the voice phenomenon and listening to some recordings that Sheargold himself had made. He told us he spends much of his spare time in the garden shed of his home in Maidenhead recording and analyzing the voices.

Sheargold felt that one very important aspect of the voice phenomenon is that it is capable of being demonstrated by anyone who is willing to investigate for himself. If voices were received only by Jürgenson, or even by Jürgenson and Dr. Raudive—but to no one else—their genuineness might be in question. But others also can obtain similar results if they will follow a few simple procedures. The initial requirements, according to him, are merely a questioning mind, a reasonably decent tape recorder, an average hearing, and a great deal of patience and perseverance.

The reality of the voices is no longer doubted by scientists who have investigated them. Only the question of their origin remains uncertain. Kjel Stenason of the Swedish State Radio says, "The voices cannot be faked. It would be impossible to do anything like it, even with all the resources of the Swedish Radio." There are three main possibilities as to the origin of the voices that have been suggested:

1. They are electronic impulses originating in the subconscious of the experimenter and registered as human speech on the tape.
2. They are transmitted by some unknown method from perhaps another planet or an intelligent source elsewhere in the universe.
3. They are people who have died on this earth and are attempting to retain communication with those

who are still here, with the voices in fact originating from where they claim they do.

It is significant that in past years certain scientists have been searching for a mechanism that would demonstrate scientifically that life after death is a reality, something similar in function to that which has produced electronic voices. Thomas Edison tried to build a machine that would contact the dead, and so did the Italian inventor Marconi.

Professor Alex Schneider, the British physicist who participated with Dr. Raudive in some of his experiments on the continent, pointed out that in seeking scientific proof of human survival of death, all that is necessary is to prove the genuineness of one other-dimensional voice and the impossibility of its being the result of some freak reception. Nothing else would be needed. His argument was similar to that of William James and his white crow. According to James, if a person should set out to show that not all crows are black, he does not have to prove that there are no black crows; but simply to produce one white crow.

In demonstrating that life goes on after death, it is not necessary to hear a thousand dead persons carry on long conversations on the tapes; all that is needed is to definitely and unmistakably produce one instance of a deceased person speaking one sentence, or even one word, from beyond death. Do this and the dogma of materialism—that nothing ever reaches us except through the physical senses—is out from here on.

It is evident that the magnetic voices will have great importance for organized religion. The Roman Catholic hierarchy already regards them as important. Since the last Vatican Council, the Catholic Church, of which both Jürgenson and Dr. Raudive are members, has shown an active interest in psychic research. It is not generally known that the Vatican has its own parapsychological research establishment.

In his work as a film producer, Jürgenson had a close connection with the pope and the Holy See for more than a decade. In this way, he came to know a number of the cardinals and other dignitaries in the Vatican to whom he introduced the voice phenomena. In 1969 he was decorated by Pope Paul VI for his achievement in discovering the voices and given the Commander's Cross of the Order of St. Gregory the Great.

One of the Vatican leaders with whom Jürgenson became close was the eminent theologian and psychologist the Reverend Dr. Gebhard Frei. Dr. Frei was cofounder of the Jung Institute in Zürich and president of the International Society of Catholic Parapsychologists; he was a man esteemed for his scholarly achievements and recognized by his church as an expert in the field of depth psychology. A short time before his death, he wrote Dr. Raudive a letter in which he said, "I feel obligated to express my gratitude for the great pains you have taken in making the first steps into uncharted land. All that I have read and heard forces me to assume that the only hypothesis able to explain the whole range of the phenomenon is that the voices come from transcendental, individual entities. . . . Whether it suits me or not, I certainly have no right to doubt the reality of the voices."

Up to the present time, there has been no official opinion expressed with regard to the voice phenomenon. However, the attitude of the Roman Catholic church toward psychic research, as we have already noticed, has been encouraging in recent years. The Holy Father's judgment of electronic voices seems to have been succinctly expressed in a statement issued from the Vatican's Research Center, which reads as follows: "To us, this is confirmation and evidence that there is a soul, that life continues, and that science may one day supply us with data and facts which may bear out the truth of our faith."

eight

Astral Projection or Out-of-Body Experiences

Everyone accepts the fact that man has a body, but it is less widely recognized that man in reality has two bodies. These are a flesh-and-blood organism and also an invisible, or astral, body that is an exact counterpart or likeness of the perfect physical body. The astral body is the directing and controlling power of the physical mechanism and is also the vehicle of operation of the personality after death.

These two bodies always separate at death; sometimes they can be separated from each other while the person is living. In this case, the individual is aware that his real conscious self is apart from his physical body and can look on it as one might view an old, castoff garment. These detachments, or projections, generally happen only once in a lifetime, but in some cases they may come more often. They usually are involuntary; frequently they

140

are life-changing. William Dudley Pelley's "Seven Minutes in Eternity," quoted in chapter 1, is a typical example of this sort.

Following the publication of the article dealing with Pelley's out-of-body journey, the author and publishers of *The American Magazine* received a flood of mail comparable to that received by Colonel Charles Lindbergh following his flight to Paris. So overwhelming was the response that it required the services of a staff of secretaries almost a year to answer the thousands of letters from people throughout the country. This avalanche of mail was divided into three broad categories.

The first group was made up of letters of commendation from people thanking him for the hope and inspiration his article had brought them. The second was from those requesting additional information concerning his sensations and reactions in respect to this and that, particularly asking for more light on the details of survival. The third group was the big surprise. It was made up of those who stated that they themselves had undergone an experience similar to that which he had related.

Pelley was, of course, under the impression that he was the only person who had ever had such an experience. He discovered from the replies that there were literally hundreds of other such cases. In fact, four out of five persons in the third group not only stated that they had had essentially the same sensations as those Pelley described in his discarnate experience, but they went on to give additional details and descriptions about the higher planes of consciousness. He knew these reports to be true because he had witnessed them on his own adventure, although he had said nothing about them in his article.

Up to the time Pelley's story was first published, I myself had never heard of such a thing as out-of-body travel.

In more recent years, I have come to have intimate contact with more than a score of highly intelligent and responsible persons who claim to have had experiences of that sort. Ralph Knight, a former associate editor of the *Saturday Evening Post*, is one of these. In his beautifully written and fascinating book *Learning to Talk with the World Beyond*, he describes one of several such experiences he has had.[1]

"It is enough to say," writes Knight, "that my journeys into the beyond were undertaken alone, lying on my bed on soft summer evenings when no one else was at home. In short, after earnest relaxation, I—my conscious self—drifted calmly out of my body, floated pleasantly away through a misty barrier, and then during a timeless time moved about in a spiritual body in a region whose scenic beauty and the lucency of near and far suns, were indescribable. Then my self gently returned home, to the room, to my body. I was indescribably refreshed, and I strolled out into the physical night, under the stars, to adore the jewels glowing in the sky."

The man who wrote the above paragraph was not a dreamer, a screwball, or a professional medium. However, his years of responsible journalism in writing newspaper editorials had made him cautious about making in print such claims as the one above about pilgrimages beyond death. He knew the horror of the "you-idiot" letters that inevitably followed even a mild exaggeration or inaccuracy in his writings. This would tend to make him doubly cautious as to the accuracy of his claims, yet he assures us that so far as the personal experience he related is concerned "the reader can accept what I say as

---

1   Ralph Knight, *Learning to Talk with the World Beyond: An Introduction to the Joy of Immortality* (Harrisburg, Pa.: Stackpole Books, 1969).

pure truth." An afternoon's visit my wife and I had with Mr. Knight in his home in Philadelphia a few years ago was sufficient to impress us with full confidence in his integrity and intelligence and the trustworthiness of his word.

Probably only a tiny percentage of the total population has ever had an experience of second body travel such as Knight describes. Yet the aggregate number of such persons is certainly far more than most people would realize. This fact has been clearly brought out since my wife and I have moved to our present home in the Southwest. Within a small New Mexico town of some forty-five thousand people, and within a period of less than twelve months, we have come to know intimately, and through sheer coincidence, a dozen persons who tell us that they have had out-of-body experiences, now commonly referred to as OBEs.

All of them are stable, trustworthy persons of high character and reliable judgment. They have given us written accounts of the occurrences, from which we shall later quote. Most of these persons assured us they had never told their strange experience to anyone before, for they did not want "to be thought queer or crazy."

The study of astral travel as a form of psychic phenomena has been curiously neglected.[1] Frederic W. H. Myers, nearly a century ago, published several instances of self-projection drawn from his paper in the "Proceedings of the British Society for Psychical Research." With

---

1   Many useful books on astral projection have been published since the author made this comment, notably: Robert Monroe's *Far Journeys* (Doubleday, 1985), *Ultimate Journey* (Doubleday, 1994); Robert Peterson's *Out-of-Body Experiences* (Hampton Roads, 1997); and Robert Bruce's *Astral Dynamics: A NEW Approach to Out-of-Body Experiences* (Hampton Roads, 1999).

this exception, the subject had hardly been discussed up to a quarter of a century ago; however, within the past few years, certain researchers have begun to investigate it seriously, and a small body of literature on the subject has been created.

The most prolific writer on the subject at present is Robert Crookall, Ph.D., a retired geologist with whom we spent an afternoon some years back at his home in Dursley, England. At the time of our visit, he had published several volumes on the subject and had greatly added to knowledge of the phenomenon through his analytical study of several hundred cases from the past and present.

Dr. Crookall's work has been largely that of collecting and analyzing the experiences of others; however, there are relatively few individuals who have themselves had frequent projections and have devoted the greater part of their lives to exploring the nature of the second body. One such person who has had extensive out-of-body experiences and has written in depth upon the subject is Sylvan Muldoon, whose valuable book *The Projection of the Astral Body* is the most authoritative study of the nature and mechanics of astral travel yet written.[1]

Muldoon's first experience took place when he was a child of twelve and was of an unexpected and harrowing nature. One night he awoke in a powerless condition, unable to see or hear or move. He was terrified, not knowing anything of the significance of what was happening to him. His body was vibrating at a great rate of speed and it seemed he was having a horrible nightmare in total darkness. He tried to move but found he could not.

---

1   Sylvan Muldoon and Hereward Carrington, *The Projection of the Astral Body* (New York: Rider, 1968).

Gradually, his sight and hearing were restored and he became aware that he was floating in the air, rigidly horizontal, a few feet above the bed. He had mysteriously begun to defy gravity. It was too unnatural for him to understand, yet too real to deny. About six feet above the bed, as if the movement had been conducted by an invisible superpower, he was uprighted from the horizontal position to the perpendicular and placed, standing, on the floor of the room.

At this point, the controlling force relaxed somewhat; except for the tension on the back of his head, he felt free. He managed to turn around, and there on the bed he saw his own body. He began to think himself insane. The two identical bodies were joined by an elastic-like cable about six feet long, one end of which was fastened to the medulla oblongata region of the astral counterpart; the other end was centered between the eyes of the physical counterpart. His first thought was that he had died during his sleep, not knowing at that time that death comes only with the severing of the elastic cable.

Struggling under the magnetic pull of the cord, he staggered toward the room in which his parents were sleeping to let them know of his awful plight. When he tried to open a door, he passed right through it. He went from one room to another, trying frantically to arouse the sleeping occupants of the house. He clutched at them, called to them, and tried to shake them, but his hands passed through them as though they were vapors. All of his senses seemed normal, save that of touch. He could not make "touchable" contact with things as before. An automobile passed by the house; he could see it and hear it plainly. The clock struck two and, looking, he saw it registered the hour.

Bewildered, Muldoon walked about aimlessly for fifteen minutes and then he noticed a pronounced increase in the resistance of the cable. It was pulling with an increasingly stronger tug and he found that he was being pulled backward toward his physical body. Again, he found himself powerless to move and in the grip of a tremendous, unseen, directing power that pulled him back to a horizontal position, directly over his bed. It was the reverse procedure of what he had experienced while rising from the bed. Slowly, the phantom lowered and then dropped suddenly, coinciding with the physical counterpart once more.

At the moment of coincidence, every muscle of Muldoon's physical mechanism jerked and a penetrating pain, as if he had been split open from head to foot, shot through him. He was physically alive again, fearful and amazed, but knowing that he had been conscious throughout the entire occurrence.

Naturally, the child had no explanation for such bewildering events and there was no one, not even his parents, to whom he could go for help or enlightenment. He continued to have repeated projections for a period of twelve years before he accidentally came on a single piece of literature on the subject by a French writer and knew, for the first time in his life, that there were other persons who had undergone similar experiences.

The evidence for the existence of some sort of second body has accumulated in recent years. Dr. Karlis Osis, in his work with the American Society for Psychical Research, says that the central hypothesis of his research is that man has an exosomatic (literally, "out of the body") aspect capable of operating independently of and away from the physical body. Startling evidence of this fact is now coming from scientists in the Soviet Union. Six Russian doctors have announced their discovery that in addition to his physical body, man has an energy body. According to them, all living things—plants, animals and human beings—not only have a physical body made of atoms and molecules, but also a counterpart body of energy. This they call the biological plasma body. The possibility has been suggested that it is the luminescence from this second body radiating outward that some claim can be seen as the human aura.

The discovery of this energy field surrounding all living objects was the outcome of what is now called Kirlian photography, a high-frequency photography discovered in 1939 by David Kirlian, a Russian engineer. A fascinating account of this is given in Ostrander and Schroeder's *Psychic Discoveries behind the Iron Curtain*.

While watching a patient receive treatment under an instrument for electrotherapy, Kirlian noticed tiny flashes of light between the electrodes and the patient's skin and decided he would try to photograph them. He placed his hand in this high-frequency field and photographed it. Lights would flash and sparkle from the hand like a display of fireworks. He placed a fresh leaf under the lens, and the edges of the leaf would light up and flash in the same way as the human body. It was found that the signals of the inner state of the organism were reflected in the brightness or dimness of the colors of the flares. A healthy person or leaf had colored lights different from those of a diseased one.

Through the electromagnetic photography it was observed that if part of the physical body is cut away, the bioplasmic body remains, clearly visible. In the Ostrander-Schroeder book, the authors relate how one of the Soviet scientists working with Kirlian photography showed them two pictures of the same leaf. The first was a large picture of a plant leaf highly magnified, a mass of sparkling lights radiating out of its edges. The second was identical with the first, except for the fact that there was a line down the middle of the right side of the leaf. As it turned out, the second was the same as the first except that the actual leaf had been cut, one third being removed. However, the energy pattern of the whole was still there. In other words, the viewer was actually seeing the "ghost" of part of the leaf, a phantom counterpart of pure energy.

Several decades before the development of Kirlian photography, some highly valuable experiments were made by a group of amateur investigators in the United States, experiments that yielded results strikingly similar in nature to those the Russian scientists have produced. The experiments took place in the 1920s when a group of eight individuals from different parts of the country gathered in New York for a month. The eight were close personal friends; four of them were highly mediumistic. The four couples, who met in the home of one of their number, included Stewart Edward White and his psychically endowed wife, Betty; Margaret Cameron, the author of *The Seven Purposes*; and Darby and Joan, the anonymous authors of *Our Unseen Guest*.[1] The meetings were probably the first time in history when a powerful psychic battery of four strong, nonprofessional mediums worked together under controlled conditions.

White's account of these sittings appeared in *The Betty Book*. Betty possessed a unique mediumship that enabled her, while blindfolded and lying quietly on a couch, to experience a kind of double consciousness. One part of her was aware of messages being relayed to another part of her from what she called the "Invisibles." Joan, whose real name was Ruth Finley, possessed com-

---

1   Margaret Cameron, *The Seven Purposes: An Experience in Psychic Phenomena* (New York: Harper and Brothers, 1918); *Our Unseen Guest* (Los Angeles: Borden Publishing Company, 1943).

parable psychic abilities. At each of the eleven experiments carried out by the group, both Joan and Betty went into a semitrance; through them, the discarnates gave directions as to the proper procedures. The goal, Joan and Betty were told, was to physically demonstrate the actual existence of the "Beta body," presumably their term for the astral or biological plasma body.

One evening Joan, blindfolded and in a deep trance, suddenly cried out sharply, "Pinch it! Feel the cold stratum." A clearly defined current of very cold air a few inches wide and extending out from Joan several feet in to the room was readily distinguishable. It appeared to be a projection of the Beta body. When Joan told them to pinch her out there in the cold stream, it was because she was presumably outside her physical body and located in the cold spot. A member of the group pinched Joan and when they did so, Joan winced and cried out with pain, as though her physical body had been pinched.

On a following evening, one of the discarnates told the group that what they were trying to do was to get Joan to allow the Beta body to go out at her fingers and that they could probably see the emanations if they squinted their eyes. "We squinched our eyes," White wrote, "and saw a faint smoke-like emanation from the ends of the fingers. This increased in density so that shortly everyone in the room could see it plainly with the eyes normal. It was a fine bluish smoke, much like cigarette smoke, but with apparently a slight phosphorescent tinge. The ordinary electric lights were on in the room.

"This and the succeeding phenomena were seen by everybody, and in most cases from several angles; at distances of from six to eight feet, to a close examination with a few inches. After everybody had determined this, a forearm began to form parallel to and about five or six inches above Joan's physical forearm. . . . For perhaps three or four seconds, the wrist and the hand were also visible to some of us. All present, however, saw the forearm, which lasted for perhaps two minutes or so."

On another evening, White relates that a smokelike substance rose from Joan's thumb and fingers until a complete outline of a double hand was visible about four inches above and to the left of her physical hand. Shortly thereafter, a nimbus began to form along the entire forearm, radiating out some two inches from the flesh. Joan was then instructed to stand up and her entire body, including the head and forearm, now formed exactly like the forearm second image.

"Cass, Darby, and I remarked at the same instant that the face was slightly out of profile. The figure was constant, but the profile was out and in; that is to say, it appeared and disappeared momentarily. Anne instructed someone to 'pinch her.' I pinched this second body at various points, and got quick and strong reactions from Joan's physical body (about eighteen inches distant) from corresponding points—knee, arm, shoulder, head."

Several centuries before Christ, Aristotle seems to have anticipated the findings of the White group of experimenters, for he held the view that one's senses can be stimulated at a distance from the physical body. He wrote, "The spirit body (second body) contains in it all of the senses."

Numerous other curious phenomena took place during the experiments with Joan's Beta body. Sometimes Joan's skin would become self-luminous, shining with a soft white light suggestive of the "altered" countenance of Jesus on the Mount of Transfiguration. At times her right hand would lengthen to twice its normal length; a luminous mistlike mask would form in front of her face or body. At other times, her physical body would seem to black out and become invisible for half a minute at a time. The thing that gave special importance to the experiments carried out by this group of amateurs was that they were done by nonprofessional mediums, with no axe to grind or preconceived notions to uphold. They were done with an unbiased interest intent on exploring significant human phenomena.

A number of our personal friends and acquaintances have furnished us with written descriptions of out-of-body experiences they have had. There are two aspects that characterize all of these reports: (1) no two of them are precisely identical, as certain details differ; (2) there are striking similarities among many of them, as certain common elements appear again and again. These aspects will be observed in each of the following reports.

The first case is that of Elizabeth, an elderly lady who in earlier years developed a blood clot on her lung at the birth of her child and was in critical condition and great pain. During her operation, she became aware that she was away from her body. She looked back on the doctors and nurses working with her but could feel no pain. Then she found herself outside in some open area, though she could see no trees. She saw her father, mother, and sister, all of whom had died some years before. She moved toward them but her mother said, "You must go back. Your family needs you." Then she reentered the operating room. Her husband was crying and she knew that she must stay with him. Then she found herself back in her body once more and she could again feel pain.

The second case is that of Joan, the middle-aged wife of a minister who had entered the hospital for a kidney test. Because she was allergic to the injections, she became critically ill. Her pulse was almost gone and her heart had virtually stopped beating. At first, while she was lying on the X-ray table, she was aware of the doctors and nurses about her. But soon she left her body and felt herself "sitting on a shelf in the upper corner of the room and just looking back and seeing all the things that were being done." She said she could hear them talking but nothing phased her. "Where I was, it didn't bother me a bit, for I was happy and had no pain."

Another such example is that of Bobby, a retired colonel in the Air Force and a member of my wife's family, who at the age of eleven had an appendectomy. His earliest conscious recollection was one of being alone in the hospital room and wanting a drink of water. "At one period, I distinctly remember standing in or near the far corner of the room and looking at myself lying on the bed. I gazed around at other parts of the room in a somewhat detached, curious way, not really concerned about seeing myself lying in a bed some six feet from where I knew I was standing.

"At subsequent periods of awareness, I remember seeing my body on the bed, but I was not too concerned about it. Some of the sensations of near weightlessness have occurred on other occasions. The ones I best remember were those that happened while I was in the Philippines as a Marine and also while in Vietnam as an F-4 pilot. These all took place at a near-sleep state, but I do not remember many of the details. I have never deliberately tried to cause these sensations to occur."

The three preceding examples from personal friends took place in connection with hospital operations, as did the famous case of Henry Hardwicke, a well-known American physician of several years back. Dr. Hardwicke's out-of-body experience had a humorous aspect and took place while he was undergoing a serious glandular operation on his throat in a North Carolina hospital. After the operation, the doctor jokingly told of getting his consciousness out of his body during the surgery and of wandering around through the rooms and corridors of the hospital, inspecting the cases and conditions of other patients.

When he ultimately came back to his body after the surgery had been dressed, Dr. Hardwicke put three of the nurses and other doctors into a dither by commenting on or discussing outstanding cases in the rooms on the floors above. "The woman in four-seventeen needs to have more attention," he advised the doctor who visited him half an hour later. "Blood poisoning seems to be setting in, and you should begin applying serums at once." "How do you know anything about the woman in four-seventeen?" the astonished physician demanded. "Because I got out of my body and went through most of the rooms," returned Dr. Hardwicke, "while you were down here cutting my throat."

A somewhat different type of projection was that of our young friend Don, who at the time of the incident was about twelve years of age. He and his brother Jay got into a good-natured scuffle in the kitchen. Jay had his arms around Don's neck and seemingly shut off either the circulation to the heart or the supply of oxygen to his lungs. As a result, Don lost consciousness and blanked out for a brief time. Jay screamed for his mother, who rushed into the kitchen to find Don lying on the floor. They soon revived him.

A few minutes later, Don said, "Mother, that was really a funny experience I had. I saw Daddy while I was out." His father had been dead for four years. He then went on to relate what took place during his unconsciousness. "At first, everything was black with a slight purple mist. Then the scene opened upon a green, grassy hill protected by a white picket fence. On the other side of the fence were many people, children and adults, running, frolicking, and having a good time. I thought to myself that it looked like such fun that I would join them.

"When I got to the gate and was about to open it, I saw Daddy standing on the other side. I said, 'Hello' and asked him if I could come in. He said, 'No, it is not your time yet.' I then begged him to allow me to enter and again he gave me the same reply, that it was not my time yet. He seemed so peaceful and real standing there that I felt if I had reached out, I could have touched him. Then the scene disappeared and everything was black again. A sensation like that of electricity went through my body and I felt as if a part of me was being lifted out of a hole. Then I found myself back in my body once more."

The next example is that of Kathleen, a teacher of Spanish at New Mexico State University at Las Cruces. "It was in 1960, a year before my mother's death. I was working very hard with my students and committee work at the university. Because I previously had had heart surgery, the doctor thought I might be overexerting myself and prescribed a tranquilizer for me. That evening I took a teaspoonful of the green liquid and sat down at my desk to grade papers.

"Very soon, I began to experience a strange sensation, which I hesitate to call sensation because it seemed so real. I was floating somewhere up near the ceiling and looking at myself sitting slumped over at the desk, still trying to grade papers. I became extremely alarmed and rushed into the bathroom. I recall that I kept thinking, 'I must get back into my body. There is no one else to take care of Mom.'

"When I got to the bathroom, I was convinced that if I looked into the mirror over the washbowl that I would not see anyone, for my body was sitting out there at the desk in the living room. Nevertheless, I forced myself to look into the mirror, and there I was, very pale, my eyes wide open and staring blankly back at me. It was a great relief to know that at least I could still make a reflection." Kathleen's experience at this point is unusual. Most projectionists, while before a mirror in their astral bodies, do not see any reflection.

"The thought that I must get back in my body was very strong, and I continued to repeat it, or think it, trying to force myself back into the body reflected in the mirror. At last, I realized that I had succeeded and went back to my paper grading. When I told the doctor about all this, he laughed and told me to discontinue the medicine and said that evidently I could not tolerate tranquilizers."

James, a twenty-year-old man, presently employed by the wastewater facility of our city as a night watchman, describes an astral projection he had that has some special features about it. His experience might suggest the phenomenon of bilocation, or being seen in two places at the same time. On this occasion, he went to bed one night and, after a period of restlessness, dropped off to sleep. The next thing he recalls is being at the wastewater plant and actually looking across at one of the primary sedimentation tanks. He was able to see the discharge of sludge from the wasting pump through the supernatant line.

Then there came over him a sense of fear that what he was visualizing was not a dream but reality. He said he had the feeling of actually seeing all these things as he would see them in his waking moments. Following this, he was not conscious of his reentry into his physical body, but he felt tremendous vibrations and a very strong roar in his ears. This frightened him and made him wonder if he were actually dying.

When he went back to work a couple of nights later, he told his buddy, also a night watchman, about his strange experience. His friend was shocked and said, "You shouldn't have told me this. You frighten me, for I saw you here at four o'clock night before last." James's friend went on to relate how, on that night, he was walking near the storage building for his four o'clock checkup of the plant and saw a figure walking on the sidewalk next to the sedimentation tank. He called to him but received no response. He tried to intercept the visitor on the opposite side of the tank, but when he got there, he saw no one.

He then made the following notation in his log: "At four o'clock, I saw someone inside the plant, but apparently there was no tampering." When James asked what clothes the man had on, his friend said, "You were wearing your usual heavy blue coat and regular uniform."

Joy, the mother of the young man employed by the water company, also had a projection that was of great significance to her. She relates how she once received a terrific blow on her mouth that shattered several teeth. Later, the mouth became infected and it was necessary to have dental surgery. The doctor gave her Pentothal, not knowing that she was allergic to it. Shortly after the injection, it seemed that her face was on fire and she began screaming frantically. For a time, the pain was so desperate she felt she was burning up.

Then she became aware that she was no longer on the table but was gliding upward into glorious pink clouds and hearing indescribably beautiful voices singing. She began to talk to herself, "Look, it's beautiful! Hear them singing. It's so beautiful. If I look back, I'll go back, and I don't want to go back." But in spite of her inner protest, she went back and found herself once more on the table fully conscious of all around her.

In evaluating her experience, Joy wrote: "This took place twenty-one years ago and the experience is just as real today as when it happened. It has left me with no doubt that life does continue after death and that there is a world beyond this world with a beauty that no language can describe. Love is all around us, and the Lord let me touch it for a moment of my life. As I recovered from the ordeal, I told one of the nurses in the operating room that I had been awake during the surgery. She denied that I was awake; when I described to her the complete conversation that took place, she went white with shock and agreed that what I heard was what took place in the operating room."

There are numerous factors that may bring about an astral projection. Most of the time our energy body remains synchronized within the physical body, but under certain conditions, it may be spontaneously ejected. This may occur when the subject is asleep, while in a coma or under the influence of an anaesthetic, or as the result of sudden shock or extreme suffering. Conversely, it may come as it did to William Dudley Pelley or Ralph Knight, while they were relaxed and resting, for no apparent reason in the world.

In Joy's case, it was the unbearable pain that seemed to have triggered her projection. The classic example of this type of exit is that of Ed Morrell, a convict who served time in an Arizona prison during the early part of the century. Morrell's account was published in his book, *The Twenty-Fifth Man*; his intimate friend Jack London fictionalized those experiences in the novel *The Star Rover*.[1]

The standard punishment for intractable prisoners at the time of Morrell's imprisonment was to truss them up in two straight jackets, one tightly laced within the other. Water was then poured over the jackets, which proceeded to shrink, causing the prisoner to feel as if he were being "slowly squeezed to death by a boa constrictor." Few of the inmates ever withstood the horrible ordeal.

---

1   Ed Morrell, *The Twenty-Fifth Man* (New York: Vantage Press, 1955); Jack London, *The Star Rover* (New York: The Macmillan Company, 1915).

At Morrell's first torture, the pain soon became intolerable. For thirty minutes, his heart pounded like sledge hammers; the cords in his neck seemed ready to burst; his breath was forced from his body and he experienced the sensation of smothering. Suddenly, he ceased to feel the pain. The walls of the prison seemed to fade out; and the next instant, he found himself outside the prison walls roaming the countryside, completely free. Morrell was repeatedly subjected to these excruciating tortures; however, as soon as the pain reached a certain intensity, he ceased to feel it. His jailers were baffled and enraged. Time and again they would come to his cell, flash the light on his face, and see him apparently sleeping soundly. Aside from a white foam that covered his lips, they could detect nothing unusual. Following these unsuccessful attempts to break his spirit, his punishments were carried to unheard-of lengths. On one occasion, he remained for 126 continuous hours under constriction. And always, after the first few horrible moments, the pain ceased and he felt a delightful release.

During these out-of-body excursions, Morrell saw and later described not only the physical body that he left but many things actually happening at the time that he could not possibly have seen physically. Imprisoned in an underground cell, with no windows, and unable to converse with anyone except his brutal jailers, he had no normal means of knowing what was taking place in the outside world. And yet, what he described so convincingly proved to be accurate upon later investigation.

It took four years for Morrell to gain his full release. During the last part of his sentence, he was not given the jacket treatment. During these last peaceful months, he tried on many occasions to project his consciousness beyond the prison walls, but he failed to do so. Try as he would, he could never detach himself and see the outer world. Apparently, one of the necessary conditions for the release of his astral body was the painful stress of being encased in the jackets. Only in his misery could he be given help.

Here is a further example of how widespread astral travel has become. An intimate friend, to whom my wife and I had recently mailed a copy of George Ritchie's *Return from Tomorrow*, told us that she was so fascinated with Dr. Ritchie's book that she read it from cover to cover as soon as her copy arrived. Then, to our surprise, she told us that she herself once had an out-of-body experience.

"For years I never breathed a word of my own out-of-body experience for fear people would think I was crazy. I was quite relieved when the subject began to be discussed in popular literature. My experience was nothing as dramatic as Dr. Ritchie's. I never left the hospital. I perched up on the curtain around the bed watching with great interest as the doctors and nurses worked on my body on the bed. Then I started down a long hall toward a beautiful beckoning light. There was a glass wall with a door, and on the other side was a beautiful garden, all green. The light was coming from somewhere in this garden.

"My father and my grandmother were on the other side of the door and my father was holding out one hand to me. At that point, my doctor, who was applying closed-heart massage, said, 'Pat, Pat, come back, your baby needs you.' I came back, slipped into my body, and I'm still here. That was almost twenty years ago. I learned two great lessons from this experience. Although I have encountered severe physical pain in the years since, I have no fear of death. And I have never ceased to marvel at the sheer goodness of life, of people, of the world; it is God's gift to us."

This final interesting case was related to us by Bob, a student at Nebraska Wesleyan University at Lincoln, Nebraska. The event he describes occurred one evening in 1970 after he had listened to the televised Nebraska-UCLA football game. Sometime after midnight, mentally exhausted, he fell quickly asleep on his bed. The next sensation he recalled was a loud, high-pitched ringing in his ears. The ringing quickly grew in intensity, as a distant wavering tone began to develop, rapidly becoming louder.

"I became frightened because of the severity of the sound. It was both inside and outside of my head. I began to feel as though my body were gently bouncing up and down, and at this point, I realized that I was totally cataleptic, not being able to distinguish the various parts of my body, let alone move them. Then all of a sudden, it felt like someone grabbed my shirt and pulled me upwards. I felt as if I were floating. I opened my eyes and saw, as I continued to float upwards horizontally, a brilliant gold light above me. Extremely frightened at this time, I thought, 'I'm dying. . . . I can't die . . . . I'm too young.' The most intense concentration of light was directly above me, but everything in the room was in a gold hue.

"At this point, as I continued to float upwards, it took a tremendous amount of effort and will to halt the motion. I tried desperately to move but could not. I noticed the room and the bed and my body below me. I saw the others sleeping. The fear and the struggle to get back continued. I felt myself fall backwards. I was in my body again, but I still couldn't move and was still on the verge of panic. It seemed like an eternity before I could even move my left hand.

"After mobility was again possible, I rose and walked around the room for quite some time. I didn't tell anyone what had happened for two or three months, although a week later I stumbled across a book listed in a catalogue (*The Projection of the Astral Body* by Sylvan Muldoon), which I promptly ordered and studied before I finally realized what had taken place. Since my first projection, I have had approximately one spontaneous projection per month."

Bob goes on to say that spontaneous projection seems to occur for him following excess physical or mental strain that has been continuous for several hours. Once on a trip to Europe, he traveled for twenty-four hours without sleep. On arrival in his hotel in Luxembourg, he lay down on his bed and had a projection within four or five minutes after he lay down. However, he willed himself back into his body and did not project from the room.

From his initial experience at the age of twelve, Sylvan Muldoon continued to have out-of-body experiences throughout his life. With ample opportunity to study hundreds of them at first hand, he reached the following conclusions concerning the nature and activity of man's "double." First, every human being has an astral body just as he has a heart, a brain, or a liver. In fact, this counterpart of the physical body, with which it normally coincides, is more genuinely the real self than is the physical man. When the double is projected, the senses are no longer in the physical body; they exist solely in the astral form. All a person's individuality is in the luminous phantom. It is this form that thinks, has consciousness, and acts.

Second, the controlling mechanism of out-of-body travel is a sort of elastic cord, or line of force, that connects the astral and physical bodies and across which flows the vital energy that sustains life in the unconscious body. This connecting cable is of grayish color and is capable of almost infinite extension. It is strikingly similar to the umbilical cord that connects the unborn infant to its mother and is the foundation on which the whole phenomenon is based. Whether rightly or wrongly, this elastic cable has often been identified as "the silver cord" referred to in Eccles. 12:6. Should this cord be severed, death instantly results; a main difference between astral projection and death is that the cord is intact in the former case, severed in the latter.

Because of his firsthand, critical examination of hundreds of out-of-body projections over the better part of a lifetime, Muldoon, it would seem, has a more intimate knowledge of the mechanism and workings of the silver cord than any other living person. This makes his testimony particularly impressive. Many times he succeeded in closely examining the action of the cable, whose vital structure is composed of the same material, or essence, as the astral body itself.

He found its elasticity goes beyond what one would imagine and is not comparable to any known material in its stretching qualities. The less distance that lies between the two bodies, the greater is the thickness of the astral cable and the greater is its magnetic pull. When the astral body was slightly out of coincidence, he observed that the cord was the diameter of a silver dollar. This diameter decreases in proportion to the increase of separation of the bodies, up to a given distance, when it is then at its minimum diameter. It retains this size, about that of a small sewing thread, from there to infinity.

The distances from immediate separation of the body to when the cord assumes its minimum size, Muldoon called the "range of cord activity." It usually varies from about eight to fifteen feet. Once the phantom advances beyond this cord activity range, it is relatively free and subject to its own will. Muldoon found by actual measurement that at a few inches of bodily separation, the cable was one and three-quarter inches; at ten feet, three-fourths of an inch; and at approximately fifteen feet, it would reach its minimum thickness and would hold this size to infinity.

This astral "line of force," in one respect, could be likened to a rubber cord; but in another respect, it is different. Suppose the rubber cord is held at each end and pulled out. As the length increases, the diameter will decrease and the resistance will intensify. With the astral cord, as the length increases, the diameter decreases, but the resistance becomes less.

A third conclusion Muldoon reached about astral travel was that it is the subconscious will that controls the projection of the astral body and ejects the phantom. This subconscious force functions with seemingly rational powers. Muldoon describes it as "that vast, unfathomable super-intelligence which is well nigh omnipotent."

He says, "This clever maneuvering of the astral body is one of the most striking—yes, astonishing impressions which one has, on first experiencing a completely conscious astral projection. I would not say that it is the first astonishing perception, but it is the second. The first almost staggering realization is that of being alive, as you have always known yourself, outside your physical body.

"The realization of it, when consciously projected—when looking upon one's lifeless physical shell—is almost too amazing to be accepted as true, and throws one into an almost ecstatic state. After recovering from this first staggering realization, the second visual miracle is the dextrous controlling intelligence in operation."

Since the silver cord stretches from one body to the other regardless of the distance between them, some people have expressed fear that in a state of projection, they might wander so far away that they might become lost and not be able to return to their physical bodies. Muldoon assures us that there is no need for such worry. It makes no difference whether one is inside or beyond the cord activity range; one is still under the operating subconscious will. It is impossible for a projector to get lost, for he can return to his physical body by merely willing to do so.

A fourth observation Muldoon made has to do with the three moving speeds at which the phantom travels in its out-of-body excursions. There is first the natural or normal speed, which is in use when the subject is moving about in his immediate environment. He merely walks. The second is the intermediate speed, in which the subject moves along without effort, faster than the normal speed, but not fast enough to cause loss of perception. This intermediate speed enables the subject to cover considerable distances rapidly, without loss of consciousness. The feet seem to glide or skim over the surface of the ground, or to be at most only a few feet above it.

The third speed is the supernormal traveling velocity, which is a speed beyond comprehension. It always occurs when the subject is unconscious and is in play when the phantom is moving back and forth over great distances. It would be utterly impossible to consciously move across a vast area at such speed and be able to realize the distance, for the conscious mind is too slow in its thinking; before it could formulate a single thought, the objective would already be reached.

Muldoon points out that while the subconscious mind can intervene in the twinkling of an eye and pull back the phantom instantly, from any distant place, into its physical counterpart, one of the inconveniences of astral projection is that too sudden a return to the physical body may create a shock and can be extremely painful. He had discovered that during sleep, in order to become the better magnet of universal energy and recharge itself more quickly, the phantom body often moves slightly out of coincidence with its physical counterpart. Muldoon found that when a person is greatly fatigued or in deep slumber, a sudden jar or loud noise can shoot the phantom back into coincidence with lightning-like speed. The result of this quick reanimation can produce a sudden severe pain, "as though a sharp-bladed instrument had passed through the entire length of the body."

On reading Muldoon's description of this "penetrating pain" that accompanied his reentry into his physical body, it occurred to me that this might possibly explain a very strange and torturous experience I myself had on three or four occasions as a child of four or five. The thing that happened to me always took place on my being awakened abruptly from an afternoon nap. The extreme pain I felt on being thus awakened was as penetrating as an electric shock and as widespread and excruciating as if I had been split from head to foot by some sharp instrument. The agony usually continued for some twenty or thirty minutes and made me excessively cross. At the time, I recall wondering what it was that had hit me; but up to the present, I have had no logical explanation for it. Was my experience that which Muldoon described? I am now inclined to think so.

There is a striking similarity between the descriptions of the Beta body observed by Sylvan Muldoon and by the Stewart Edward White group of investigators with that of the Soma Pneumatikon, or risen body of Jesus, described in the four Gospels. This is not to say that the two sets of phenomena are identical, but they are certainly analogous in a number of important respects. While Christian faith holds that the Resurrection of Jesus was something far more than mere phenomenalism, there are unmistakable parallels between the description of Jesus's elastic body and that of the energy body of modern psychic research. In both instances, we seem to be dealing with a material of an intermediate nature between matter and nonmatter.

The late Dr. G. N. M. Tyrrell, president of the British Society for Psychical Research, said: "Philosophers have in general assumed man to be a straightforward compound of two factors, one mental and the other material. Psychical research, however, has shown man to be nothing of the kind. It has shown that he does not consist of pure mind tacked on to pure body. He consists of a vast complex personality, which more nearly resembles a hierarchy of elements, stretching in gradation from pure self at one extreme to pure body at the other. Some of these elements appear to be neither mental nor physical but to possess a character midway between the two."

It is evident in the Gospel records that Jesus's Resurrection was no hallucinatory event that existed only in the minds of his disciples, as some regard it, nor was it the resuscitation of a corpse, a dead man come back to life. It was something distinctively different to either of these options. Notice Luke's description of Jesus's appearance to his disciples on the first Easter evening: "As they were talking above all this, there he [Jesus] was, standing among them. Startled and terrified, they thought they were seeing a ghost. But he said, 'Why are you so perturbed? Why do questionings arise in your minds? Look at my hands and feet. It is I myself. Touch me and see; no ghost has flesh and bones as you can see that I have.' They were still unconvinced, still wondering, for it seemed too good to be true. So he asked them, 'Have you anything here to eat?' They offered him a piece of fish they had cooked, which he took and ate before their eyes" (Luke 24:36-43).

It is quite plain in this account that the risen body of Jesus had a dual quality. At one time, it was immaterial enough to pass through closed doors, or even closed tombs, without opening them; at other times, it was physical enough for his disciples to touch and handle it. The Apostle Paul describes what modern psychic research would call the two counterpart bodies when he says, "There is a natural body and there is a spiritual body."[1]

Out-of-body travel is not a recent development, although relatively few people are aware of the fact. The reaction of those who experience the phenomenon for themselves for the first time is frequently that of Sandy the Scotsman whose friends persuaded him to bet a shilling on a horse race: to his stupefaction, he won three pounds. "In the devil's name," cried Sandy, "how lang has this been going on?" Astral projection has been going on for a long time. It is a universal experience, not in the sense that it happens to a large percentage of people, but that it has happened all through recorded history from the early Egyptians to the present day.

Many of the great mystics of the church have especially been given to out-of-body travel. One of these was Emanuel Swedenborg (1688–1772), one of the incontestable geniuses of the eighteenth century. A mathematician, physicist, engineer, and philosopher, Swedenborg was highly respected as one of the intellectual giants of his time. The stupendous range of the man's intellect, together with the sheer quantity of his scientific achievements, staggers the imagination.

Swedenborg was one of the creators of the modern sciences of crystallography and metallurgy. He identified

---

1   For a fuller discussion of the nature of the risen body of Jesus, see W. M. Justice, *Our Visited Planet* (Lincoln, Nebr.: Services, 1973), pp. 73–108.

electrical phenomena nineteen years before Benjamin Franklin's experiments. He was the first anatomist to perceive correctly the functions of the ductless glands and cerebrospinal fluid. He developed the basis of the modern theory of molecular magnetics, and he anticipated the solar origin of the earth, the undulatory principle of light, and the nebular hypothesis. During the time he was engaged in these multitudinous scientific activities, he reports having many out-of-body excursions.

His great religious experience came in 1744, at the age of fifty-six, "when heaven opened to him." This resulted in a continuing series of visions and a constant awareness of the presence of God that shaped his theological writings and gave rise to the religious movement in Europe that now bears his name. While he was employed by the Swedish government as chief adviser in scientific and technical matters, Swedenborg was at the same time writing vivid descriptions of what life after death is like and describing numerous conversations he had held with spirits whom he identified as "angels."

John Wesley, the founder of Methodism, greatly admired the noble character of Swedenborg and desired an interview with him. Wesley did not speak of this wish to anyone, but to his amazement he received a letter from Swedenborg, dated February 1772, stating that he had been informed by the spirit world that Wesley wanted to see him in London. Wesley replied, giving a date some months in the future. In answering Wesley's letter, Swedenborg said regretfully he would not be able to make the appointment at the time suggested, for on the twenty-ninth of the next month he was departing this life for the spirit world. The record shows that Swedenborg's prophecy was correct, the date of his death being March 29, 1772.

Centuries before Swedenborg, the Apostle Paul wrote a letter to the church at Corinth in which he describes an out-of-body experience he once had (2 Cor. 12:1–4). So powerful was its effect on the great apostle that he described himself as being "caught up to the third heaven." Both Swedenborg and Saint Paul are outstanding examples of religious mystics who have had "visions and revelations of the Lord," but there are numerous others. Church history is full of them.

The great theologian Saint Augustine (354–430), whose work and writings have had a decisive impact on Western thought, claimed that he left his physical body on occasion. In one of his sermons, he relates how his own spiritual body was twice seen by others at a considerable distance. Saint Teresa of Avila, Saint Bernard of Clairvaux, the lady Julian of Norwich, and a host of others in the higher echelons of sainthood have had similar experiences.

The enormous number and similarity of such cases as the preceding ones reported in this chapter can no longer be ignored by thoughtful persons. Individuals, knowing nothing of anyone else's analogous experiences, will often give almost identical accounts of their own. A single instance of out-of-body travel should have the highest significance in itself alone, but the volume of such independent stories, being what it is, makes their value en masse almost staggering.

Astral projectionists such as Oliver Fox, Yram, William Gerhardi, and Caroline Larsen, who have spent years of their lives studying out-of-body phenomena, would all declare with Muldoon that there are two overwhelming impressions that invariably follow an authentic instance of astral projection: first, the magisterial reality of the experience, and second, the absolute certainty of life after death.

Those who have never experienced such things for themselves are almost sure to put the experience down to a vivid dream or attribute it to some form of mental disorder. But nobody who has had an astral projection will ever admit for a moment that such confusion is possible. The experience is life-changing and belief-compelling. As one projectionist put it, "It has no resemblance to dreaming. In a dream, one may not know he is unconscious, but when he is conscious, he does know that he is not dreaming. If the whole world united in telling me that it was a dream, I would remain unconvinced."

Out-of-body experiences represent one of the most important proofs for human survival. The logical assumption is that if the spiritual counterpart that carries the human consciousness is able to leave the physical during life, it would seem possible to do so at the time of death. Of all vital phenomena, Frederic W. H. Myers considered what he called, at that time, "self-projection" as the most significant because it is "the one definite act which it seems as though a man might perform equally well before and after death."

Because of their firsthand knowledge, the one thing all projectionists universally agree on is that it is possible to live and function consciously outside the physical body. One person who has had numerous out-of-body excursions describes it this way: "There is much that I know I don't know; therefore I classify things into three categories: the things I know, the things I believe, and the things I hope are true. The first of these is a very small amount. However, some of it is tremendously important, the most profound of which is the fact that I know that we survive this physical life. I do not say I believe it. I say I know it."

The testimony of Sylvan Muldoon, as he ends his book, is equally unequivocal: "Once you experience the projection of your astral body, you will no longer doubt that the individual can exist apart from his physical body. . . . For my part, had a book on immortality never been written, had a lecture on 'survival' never been uttered, had I never witnessed a séance or visited a medium; in fact, had no one else in the whole world suspected life after death, I should still believe implicitly that I am immortal—for I have experienced the projection of the astral body."

nine

The Nature of the After-Death Life

Granted that Sylvan Muldoon and millions of Christian believers throughout the world are right in their conviction that there is a future life, what is the nature of this after-death life? When a person dies, where does he go? If a glimpse of the world beyond is available, what are the controlling factors "over there"?

There are two principal sources from which we may derive insight as to the nature of the life after death: first, the revelation of reality found in the New Testament, particularly the teachings of Jesus and the Resurrection Event; and second, the transcendental experiences of mankind that have been recognized throughout the centuries but that only recently had been scientifically studied and investigated on a broad scale.

While life after death is a central doctrine of the Christian religion, including the Roman Catholic, the Greek Orthodox, and the Protestant churches, there is a difference of opinion in the Christian camp as to just exactly what the nature of the life is immediately following the experience of dying. An illustration of this difference was brought out at a family camping conference some years back. One of the preachers at this conference led a group discussion in which he said, "Your loved ones who are dead are not in heaven. They're asleep." Some of those present had recently buried a parent, a child, or a brother or sister; they were so shocked, surprised, and angry that they sat up all night discussing the matter.

Historically, two opposing views have been held by Christians since the early centuries concerning the present state of the dead and the nature of their life immediately following death. The first view is that the dead remain in an unconscious state until the Last Judgment, when a final resurrection takes place. This concept is embodied in some of the ancient symbolism and liturgy of the church, depicting death as a sleep and the grave as a dormitory or "sleeping place" of the soul. Certain hymns, such as "Asleep in Jesus," suggest this, as does also an ancient burial service that refers to a final awakening "when the earth and the sea shall give up their dead."

The second view is that the dead are not sleeping in the grave, but are presently living a vivid, conscious life, with mind, memory, and personality unchanged. According to this concept, dying does not destroy one's essential nature, but we pass in to the unseen world with our personalities unchanged and with our feelings, memory, intellect, and real selfhood the same as in their earthly existence.

Each of these positions has its advocates and scriptural proof and texts can be found to sustain both of them. Martin Luther taught the doctrine of soul-sleeping after death. "We are to sleep," said the great reformer, "until Christ comes and knocks on the grave and says, 'Dr. Martin, get up.'" Conversely, John Calvin strongly rebuffed the doctrine of soul sleep. He maintained that the soul truly lived after death and was embued with self-consciousness and understanding. Numerous Christian bodies have shared Calvin's view at this point. In one of its early articles of religion, the Anglican Church took a position similar to his and asserted as a cardinal belief of the church that "they which say that the souls of those who depart hence do sleep, without sense, feeling, or perceiving till the day of judgment . . . do utterly dissent from the right belief declared to us in the Holy Scriptures."

If there is one fact that seems to emerge from the acts and teachings of Jesus as recorded in the New Testament, it is that death does not destroy our personalities or change our essential characters after death. There is nothing in the words of Jesus to indicate a timeless interval of sleeping in the grave. Instead, his promise to the thief on the cross—"This day shalt thou be with me in Paradise"—suggests an immediate entry into a new state of conscious existence. In fact, the words themselves imply that Jesus made a definite promise to meet the thief on the other side of death. In doing this, he made two points perfectly clear: first, that they both would survive the death of the physical body, and second, that they would recognize each other in their new state of existence. Otherwise, the promise would lack content and would be meaningless.

A similar point can be made in the case of the rich man and Lazarus, both of whom had undergone physical death and later found themselves in an after-death state of being. Whether the story was a parable or a description of two actual persons whom Jesus had once known, the essential truth of conscious life in the beyond is the same. In both cases, the two men were represented as being in a state of clear conscious existence after death.

They were described as thinking, speaking, and feeling, with no break in memory or awareness.

It has been generally assumed that there is no possible point of contact between this world and the next that could tell us anything about what things are like on the other side of death. Shakespeare, in an oft-quoted sentence, speaks of "that undiscovered country from whose bourn no traveler returns." We have usually accepted at face value the great bard's assertion of the complete impossibility of knowing anything firsthand about the nature of things beyond death. We have ignored the fact that the greatest religion on earth is founded on the historic fact that its founder did come back from the "undiscovered" world of the dead. He made a report of it to more than five hundred of his chosen friends and disciples, the wonder of which radiates throughout the New Testament. If we would know what the after-death state is like, we cannot leave Jesus and his teachings out of the picture.

In addition to the witness of Jesus and the New Testament, a second source of information about the life ahead is the reports of persons having near-death, or out-of-body, experiences who have returned to describe what things they have seen and heard. Dr. Raymond A. Moody, in his valuable study *Life after Life*, has collected accounts of more than a hundred and fifty such cases.[1] He has interviewed in great detail some fifty persons who were resuscitated after having been pronounced clinically dead by the doctors. Since making his initial study, Moody has extended his collection of near-death cases to more than three hundred, and this list is growing rapidly.

---

1   Raymond A. Moody, *Life after Life* (Harrisburg, Pa.: Stockpile Books, 1976).

Also, Dr. Elisabeth Kübler-Ross, in her work with terminally ill patients, has been pursuing the same research, and getting essentially the same results. She has accumulated several hundred such reports. These extraordinary experiences of people who have crossed the brink of death and have returned can shed much light on the nature of the life ahead.

Among the outstanding cases reported in recent years is the experience of Dr. George Ritchie Jr., a distinguished physician and psychiatrist who was pronounced dead by his doctors but miraculously returned to life to tell of an incredible glimpse he had had of the world beyond death. The case has attracted widespread attention and has provided some of the most startling, yet most helpful, descriptions of the realms beyond our own that have been brought to light in this century.

Some months ago my wife and I had the pleasure of being overnight guests of Dr. Ritchie and his wife in their lovely Virginia home on the Chesapeake Bay. We listened spellbound as our host related to us his astonishing story of out-of-body travel. What he described to us during our visit, embodied in his fascinating book *Return from Tomorrow*, is probably destined to exercise a shaping influence on many person's conceptions of what the after-death life is like.

Dr. Ritchie's experience, which one of his doctors described as "the most amazing medical case I ever encountered," took place during World War II while Dr. Ritchie was in military training at Camp Barkeley, Texas. He had been selected to return to the Medical College of Virginia in Richmond, Virginia, for training as an army doctor. But just before he was to leave for Richmond, he came down with a critical case of double lobar pneumonia and was taken to the hospital. While being X-rayed, he collapsed to the floor and was taken back to his room, where he remained unconscious for five days. During this period, twice in the course of nine minutes his doctors pronounced him dead. Dr. Ritchie's description of what took place during the interval of his unconsciousness had qualities in common with other out-of-body experiences. He saw his physical body lying at a distance from his conscious self. He was unable to make touchable contact with physical objects. He went through material walls as though they did not exist. But the thing that gave his experience its high significance was his meeting with a Being of Light, whom he identified as the Christ. "There is no word in our language," said Dr. Ritchie in relating the story to us, "to describe a brilliance so intense. The light that entered the room that night was Christ: I knew because a thought was put deep within me, 'You are in the presence of the Son of God.'" The overwhelming impression of the divine figure described by Ritchie was that of "absolute, indescribable love." He then went on to say, "The best way I can state this is to say I was in the presence of a Being who knew everything about me, good and bad, and yet totally accepted and loved me. Never have I been in the presence of such absolute, pure love. Never have I been in the presence of such total wisdom."

The presence of the Radiant One brought something else into the hospital room that night. Every episode of Dr. Ritchie's life passed before him in a series of pictures. All the major events of his twenty years of life were there and passed before his vision as vividly real as images on a screen. Each picture came in answer to a single question, "What have you done with your life?" In the light of the divine Presence, Dr. Ritchie's record seemed shoddy and inadequate.

Following this panoramic view of his past life, Dr. Ritchie was taken on a journey and, like the poet Dante, was given a glimpse of three areas of the universe. The first of these areas might be described as the Realm of the Bewildered Spirits, where the discarnate, earth-bound entities, enslaved by their perverted desires and appetites, congregated. The second was controlled by a higher order of interest, of beings engaged not in self-worship but in an impersonal search for truth. The third was a far-off glimpse of the ultimate heaven, a City of Light populated by transformed beings who had taken on the likeness of the King of Light.

Led by the Being of Light, Ritchie entered the first of these areas after what he described as "moving high above the earth, speeding toward a distant pinprick of light." It was a large city, late at night, and many buildings had lights burning on every floor. There was something strange about the focus of Dr. Ritchie's vision, for he could see ordinary buildings, but he could see other buildings through them.

Dr. Ritchie followed the Being of Light through crowded streets and country lanes. Everywhere he saw this other existence strangely superimposed on the familiar world. While the streets and offices were crowded with a host of discarnate entities, those still living in their physical bodies were totally unaware of their presence. Dr. Ritchie saw men and women working at their desks, while standing behind them were other astral beings trying to communicate with them as they worked. In one section of the realm where the astral and the physical overlapped, he saw a discarnate female following a man, probably her son, instructing him as to how to live his life, but he couldn't hear her. "Was this what death was like—to be permanently invisible to the living, yet permanently wrapped up in their affairs?" Dr. Ritchie wondered.

It became evident to Dr. Ritchie that these earth-bound spirits whom he encountered on his strange journey had retained all the sordid cravings and appetites they had had on earth, but they no longer had the power to satisfy them. In a squalid area of the city, they entered a dingy saloon. A large crowd of people lined the bar three deep, while others jammed the wooden booths along the wall. Dr. Ritchie noticed that a number of men standing at the bar were unable to lift their drinks to their lips. Over and over, they clutched for their glasses of whiskey, but their hands passed through the solid tumblers, through the heavy wooden countertop, and through the arms and bodies of the drinkers about them.

It was obvious that the living people—the ones actually doing the drinking and talking—could neither see the desperately thirsty discarnates among them nor feel their frantic eagerness to get at those drinks. Some of the living beings at the bar were being "possessed" by the disembodied alcoholics who jumped inside their human bodies at any moment when the electric fields or auras were relaxed and began to open. The compulsion on the part of these wretched beings was understandable.

"Presumably," said Dr. Ritchie, "these substanceless creatures had once had solid bodies, as I myself had had. Suppose that when they had been in their bodies they had developed a dependence on alcohol that went beyond the physical. That became mental. Spiritual, even. Then, when they lost that body, except when they could briefly take possession of another one, they would be totally cut off for all eternity from the thing they could never stop craving. An eternity like that . . . would be a form of hell." Up to this point in their travel, the radiant Being had taken Dr. Ritchie into a realm of earthbound spirits where the living and the dead existed side by side; now, however, they entered a deeper level of human depravity where they saw no living man or woman. The busy city was behind them and they were now standing on the edge of a vast plain crowded with hordes of ghostly discarnates. They looked out over endless miles of the most horrible sights imaginable.

Astral beings were tied up in all kinds of lewd relationships. Unmentionable sexual obscenities were being enacted all around them in feverish pantomine. The air was saturated with hate and animosity. Never had he seen such frustrated, miserable, and completely selfish human beings. Yet, working in the midst of this horrible place, unseen by most of the depraved wretches, were Beings of Light who were trying to save these people. After this, the second sphere was introduced in much the same way as the preceding one. There was a new quality of light, an increased intensity of vision, and a new realm was superimposed on the physical world; it was a "mental realm" where ego had been left behind and where everyone was engaged in a selfless search for truth.

Dr. Ritchie inferred that it was this source from which the great songs, paintings, symphonies and inventions came. In this second sphere, unlike the first, there was no absorption with self and earthly trivia; everyone seemed to be engaged in some great enterprise. He saw sculptors and philosophers, composers and inventors, who seemed to be a part of "some tremendous study center, humming with the excitement of great discovery." There were what might be described as great universities and libraries, and scientific laboratories that surpassed the wildest imagination of science fiction.

Unlike the previous "hellish" realm, filled with beings trapped in some form of self-attention, here was another kind of existence. The wretched souls of the first sphere were shut up in their hatreds and lusts, with their minds fixed on material things forever out of reach; in the second realm, there was an all-pervading peace. "Everyone we passed in the wide halls and on the curving staircases seemed caught up in some all-engrossing activity. . . . Whatever else these people might be," said Dr. Ritchie, "they appeared utterly and supremely self-forgetful—absorbed in some vast purpose beyond themselves."

Dr. Ritchie sensed that every activity on this mighty campus had its source in God, but that even this was not the ultimate, "that He had far greater things to show me if only I could see."

Of the third, or ultimate, heaven, only a glimpse was given. Dr. Ritchie and his guide no longer seemed to be on the earth but were immensely far away. In the infinite distance, Dr. Ritchie saw a city of pure light, if such a thing is conceivable, in which the walls, houses, and pinnacles seemed to give off light. "I did not see any golden streets," he said, "but what I did see was even more amazing. The beings that came and went from this city of pure light were like the Being who was conducting me. He did say, 'I am the first fruit of many who are to follow.' Two of those beings from this glorious city started toward us and the whole thing was gone. We were suddenly back in the hospital room in Texas."

Dr. Ritchie's experience has turned out to be one of the most detailed and convincing glimpses of the nature of the after-death life on record. If his case were the only one in existence, it would in itself be highly significant; even more important, however, is the fact that Dr. Ritchie's experience is not solitary. Hundreds of other persons have had close calls with death and have come back with remarkably similar accounts.

Descriptions from the more than three hundred persons Dr. Raymond Moody interviewed, all of whom had been clinically dead or had had near-death experiences, contained certain common features. In fact, the similarities were so great that he picked out fifteen parallel elements that occurred repeatedly in the mass of narratives he had collected. No two cases were precisely identical and no one person reported every single component of the experience, but numerous persons reported that they had had most of them. These common features were present not only in the descriptions of the mechanics of dying but also in the reports of the nature of life after death that the subjects brought back with them.

The case of Arthur Ford, probably the most widely known and effective trance medium of our generation, is strikingly similar in many of its features to that of Dr. Ritchie's. While I heard Ford lecture on two occasions and once had a luncheon engagement with him in a New York hotel, I never had the opportunity of attending one of his séances. Oddly enough, with all his psychic gifts, it seems that Ford had only one experience of astral travel. He describes it, however, as the outstanding event of his career and declares that for him, it lifted the problem of personal survival "out of the realm of faith and brought it clearly down to the plane of realism."

The event, which he related in his book *Nothing So Strange*, occurred while he was critically ill in a Florida hospital.[1] Ford sensed that the doctors did not expect him to last the night and wondered how long it would take him to die.

Then he began to realize that he was floating in the air and saw his body on the bed, but he took no interest in it. He could not comprehend the nature of the body he was functioning in, but he knew his individual consciousness was outside his physical body. Then he found himself in a green valley, with mountains on every side, and every-

---

1   Arthur Ford with Margueritte Harmon Bro, *Nothing So Strange: The Autobiography of Arthur Ford* (London: Psychic Press, 1966).

where an unearthly brilliance of light and color. He saw coming towards him people he had known and thought of as dead. Some who had died in decrepit old age now gave the impression of vigorous youth; others, who had passed over as children, were in mature spirit bodies.

He missed a number of people he had expected to see and asked about them. Immediately the lights grew dim and the colors faded. The persons to whom he had been speaking faded out while those of whom he had inquired appeared in hazy shapes. He knew he was allowed to view a lower sphere. He cried out to the friends for whom he had asked and they seemed to hear, but did not reply. Then everything cleared again and a gentle radiant person stood beside him and told him not to worry about them. Ford was told these persons could come to the higher sphere any time they wanted to, if they desired it more than anything else.

Everyone that Ford saw seemed happily intent upon mysterious errands. Some persons, whom he had known well in the past, did not pay much attention to him. Others he had known only slightly, or not at all, seemed attracted to him; without explanation, he realized that in the spirit world the law of affinity determined relationships.

At one point a court of higher beings considered his condition. He wondered if these spirits could be the angels and the archangels of which the Bible sometimes speaks. They seemed to have little interest in the usual misdemeanors so frowned upon in earth society, but they were seriously concerned about the waste of valuable energy or talents and his dissipation of opportunity to accomplish what he knew he was meant to fulfill. It was made clear to him that he must go back. But he rebelled, and like a spoiled child in a tantrum, braced his feet and fought against going. Then there was a sense of hurtling through space and he found himself looking into a nurse's face in the Florida hospital. She told him he had been in a coma for two weeks.

What Arthur Ford and George Ritchie saw in their amazing journeys into the beyond convinced both of them of two crucially important facts about the hereafter: one, that consciousness does not end with physical death; in fact, it becomes keener and more alive than ever. And two, that how we occupy our time on earth, the kind of relationships we build, is tremendously more important than we realize. These two insights are common to almost everyone who has had a clinical death or out-of-body experience. Such persons are given a new sense of values and their total outlook becomes changed.

One of our friends who has had numerous out-of-body experiences was asked what effect astral projection had on his physical existence and whether it took anything out of him that made him less efficient in his everyday work. His reply was, "No, it does not, except the effect of being preoccupied. The basic problem is the dualism that makes many things all around you in the here and now mighty mundane or insignificant. One's experience 'over there' becomes more real than the here and now, and the question arises, 'Which place will get my attention?'"

This dualism could have been a problem for Lazarus after he had been restored to life through the healing power of Jesus. In his poem, *An Epistle Concerning the Strange Medical Experience of Karshish, the Arab Physician,* Robert Browning describes the changed outlook of Lazarus following his death experience and how things that seemed of great importance to others, such as a marching battalion or the erection of a magnificent building, might leave him completely apathetic, while some seeming trifle, such as a crippled bird or the laughter of a child, would appear to be of infinite import.

There are several important things to notice about the world Dr. Ritchie and Arthur Ford were shown that can give us valuable hints of the nature of the life ahead. The first of these is the Reign of Law. The great life principles function the same after death as they did before. Mercy, truth, justice, and love are operative in both the seen and the unseen worlds. Of these parallel laws, the most majestic is probably the law of cause and effect. "Whatsoever a man soweth, that shall he also reap." There is no escape from this law; it is inexorable and almost merciless in its nature. As the saying goes, "Sow a thought, reap an act; sow an act, reap a habit; sow a habit, reap a character; sow a character, reap a destiny."

In the ordinary round of daily living, the working of the law of cause and effect is not so apparent on the earthly plane as it is in the spirit life. In the latter case, it would appear to be almost a tangible thing. Betty White, in one of her excursions into the world of other-consciousness, describes the difference by saying, "Law is a thing here. It operates. And here we all understand that if we run up against a law, we bump. And the breaking of a law here has a different reaction on the individual consciousness than does the breaking there. And it's not done."

A second characteristic of the hereafter is the Law of Spiritual Openness. In the out-of-body or after-death state, it is impossible to hide one's real self from others. The astral body is so sensitive to the condition of the soul within that it manifests unmistakably one's true character. There are no hypocrites in heaven. On earth we have a facade, a mask behind which we hide; but there, the mask has disappeared and we can no longer hide behind it. Deceit cannot exist. There is no possibility of lying or concealing anything about ourselves. We are open to the knowledge and gaze of all. A patient, describing his near-death experience, said that in the out-of-body life, the fact that character and inner motives were totally apparent to everyone acted as a moral prophylactic by making one feel the need to "clean up" one's behavior.

A third characteristic involves the nature of Future Punishment. The traditional teachings of the hereafter receive very little support from the experience of those who have visited the astral plane and know something of conditions on the other side. Instead of the orthodox heaven and hell, something quite different seems to be the case. Punishment is not objective, but inherent and automatic. It is something within.

In Dr. Ritchie's case, it consisted of having a panoramic view of his past life. In the case of Ford, it was a court of higher beings that functioned as his accusing conscience. In both instances, it was, in reality, a judgment of God through their higher selves. One who had returned from a near-death experience described the "judgment to come" as being able to see ourselves as we are, and by no stretch of imagination being able to avoid it.

The question is often raised as to how a merciful God could send anyone to hell eternally. It would seem that if anyone is in hell, he has put himself there, and God only respects his free choice. A self-centered person who makes himself the center of his own world, who refuses to love anything beyond and greater than himself, would find himself very uncomfortable in heaven, for heaven is giving totally in love and being loved. All who are in hell are there because they choose to be there. They hate one another's company, but they hate the society of good spirits worse still. C. S. Lewis in his exquisite little fantasy *The Great Divorce* pictures a busload of people leaving the gray grim of hell for a journey to the radiant splendors of heaven—not liking what they found there. Only one person stayed. The others chose to go back on the return bus.

Another great law that operates in this life and in the life to come is the Law of Spiritual Affinity, in which like gravitates to like. In the earthly life, we are all mixed up together, good and bad, saints and criminals alike. In the next life, we are separated and each gravitates to his own spiritual level. Imagine what this must mean to those whose lives have been evil and who are compelled to live exclusively with people of their own kind.

One report that came back from high levels of the beyond illustrates the working of this law. It is the example of a wealthy man who, by his vices, had brought suffering and even sin into the lives of others. While the man was on earth, he was treated with some toleration on account of his wealth or his position or his abilities. But on reaching the other side, he passes on to that level and place to which he belongs because of what he is and not because of what he appeared to be, or desired to be thought. He finds himself surrounded entirely by others who have the same sins, vices, and limitations as himself.

This creates a collective condition very different from his environment on earth. Each of his associates becomes an object lesson to the others, each one is a reflection of the others. The whole atmosphere, even the scenery of the place, are colored with the hopeless drabs and grays of their mental and spiritual outlook.

The awakening, or what one would term judgment, comes to such people very slowly. At first, there is felt a resentment at being in such a condition. This is followed by bitter disappointment at being unable to buy or to enforce better conditions. Then, when they realize that they cannot command different surroundings, they begin to wonder why. At this point they wake up to the fact that something is wrong within themselves that needs to be changed. Visitors come to them from the higher spheres to show they have risen above their lower selves and deeply desire a change. This is like sending missions to the heathen. As you know, the heathen at first do not always believe what the missionaries tell them. In the same way, our visitors are not usually believed at once but may have to go to them many times before making any impression.

Eventually, however, one of them will begin to sense the contrast: "Why is it that this man or woman is so different from us? Why are they able to go away from this miserable place and return at will? How is it that they speak to us with love, sympathy, and hope, when all others are thinking only of themselves?" When this seed begins to germinate, it brings the realization "I am with these wretched people because I am of them; in fact, because I am like them." When that happens, there comes the desire to be different. Then follows the awakening of which I have spoken. It brings a bitterness and remorse that is the greatest and most terrible punishment man can have. No torture another can inflict is so terrible as the remorse one's own best self inflicts when enlightenment comes.

Although this is a terrible experience for many, running through it is a vein of hope, a feeling that one will be able to overcome and work it out, and that gives courage. Were this not so, one might be overwhelmed when realizing the truth. But there is always hope, the opportunity of recovering lost ground. And this way of recovery is in helping others who have similar limitations, difficulties, or vices.

The final law controlling the after-death life that we shall mention is the Law of Growth. It is inconceivable to believe that the life beyond is a life without continuous growth and progress. Some of the descriptions we have already noticed indicate that the acquisition of knowledge continues in the afterlife and that the present world is simply a kindergarten for higher growth beyond. Dr. Ritchie's description of schools, libraries, and institutions of learning correspond to parallel views that others have also had.

Several persons told Dr. Raymond Moody that during their encounter with "death" they got a momentary glimpse of "an entire separate realm of existence" in which all knowledge of past, present, and future seemed to coexist in a sort of timeless state. During this period, in a flash of universal insight, the individual seemed to have complete knowledge. A woman interviewed said that for a few seconds she felt that she knew "all the secrets of all ages, all the meaning of the universe, the stars, the moon—of everything" and that there was no question that did not have an answer.

She went on to say that the memory of all these things that happened remained clear, all except that fleeting moment of knowledge that disappeared when she returned to the body. From such reports as these, it is clear that learning in the higher realms of being is not a matter of individual concern alone but is for the general good of all. "We're always reaching out," said one, "to help others with what we know."

Service seems to be the goal in the hereafter. All those in the second realm, as Dr. Ritchie observed, were "absorbed in some vast purpose beyond themselves." Even in the midst of the earthbound wretches of the first realm, there were Beings of Light trying to help. It would seem that the reward of faithful workers in the hereafter is not retirement on a pension but enlarged opportunity for growth and progress.

Just what the nature of the service is that we shall do, we cannot say, but reason says that it will be in keeping with our talents and capacity, our training and growth here. "Thou has been faithful over a few things," said the

Lord to his good servant, "I will make thee ruler over many things." It seems we can hardly escape a kind of moral aristocracy in heaven, not of pride, but out of a response to grace. Some subjects said that what they saw during their near-death experience caused them to believe that the ability to love others and the accumulation of knowledge were the two most important goals to seek in life.

A friend tells us of a strange and mystical experience she once had in which she saw her true life in its large perspective. The insight changed her outlook on her mission. Her description evokes the qualities of a typical astral projection: "May I tell you a peculiar experience that happened to me one night before I went to sleep. I was not asleep, just relaxed, and seemingly I began to float away from the earth. I could see the planet getting smaller and smaller. I was just out in the navy blue [of deep space], with stars all around. It was no dream; I was totally conscious. Finally, I got so far away that I could see the earth, way down below like a little ball, marble-sized.

"All of a sudden, I realized that I was in infinity, and the most desolate sense of isolation I have ever felt came upon me. I had shrunk to the size of a single cell, floating alone in the great immensity. Then I thought to myself, 'Good gracious, this is eternity!' The awful sense of aloneness I then felt—the feeling of floating in a sea of nothingness, of having nothing to hold on to—is truly the most horrible concept of hell that could possibly be.

"I looked back down to the earth and all of a sudden I began to see a sort of panorama of the history of civilization—the great works of man, monuments for this and that, beautiful museums, books and libraries, and all the things that were of earthly greatness. All of it seemed to me as nothing, nothing. Then the idea came to me that the only really necessary thing for us to know is not intellectual learning, academics, or anything like that. The only thing of any real importance for us is learning how to communicate with that silence in which I was floating.

"Then I thought, well, I certainly have missed it because I have known about prayer, about meditation, and yet I have been too busy with the things of Caesar. At that moment, it came to me that I should begin to practice a little of what I remembered about inwardness, the going within to communicate. The minute I did this, the void of navy blue, in which I thought myself alone, was no longer empty. The emptiness in which I was floating became alive, and I could communicate with the thing I was floating in. This turned my hell into paradise. I now had the comfort of this warm, wonderful Something that enveloped me and with which I could communicate.

"Then I thought to myself, from here on I will do my things in a disciplined life and learn to go within and communicate with this so-called silence; for it is not silence, nor empty, but vital and with something of a communicative nature about it. This insight certainly revealed the contrast between the great realities and the smaller realities that people put so much store in as being of importance."

Our friend could say with William James, "We and God have business with each other; and in opening our lives to his influence, our deepest destiny is fulfilled." In her process of "going within to communicate" our friend had discovered the great secret. The essence of New Testament teachings, and the reports of those who have returned from the deeper levels of life beyond death, indicate that communion with God is the most important act of man. This is the big thing. Nothing else really matters in this world or the next.

The After-Death Experiences of William Justice

Three days after the death of my father, William Justice, I was in prayer as usual in the morning. It is my custom to write out my prayers and any questions I have for the Lord. Then I listen. Most of the time, words come in a small voice to my mind. I write these words without questioning them. Later, I examine what comes to see if it fits with the loving Spirit of Jesus as I have come to know him.

On September 2, 1985, my prayer was "Dear Father, surround me with the protective white light of Christ so that I will hear your words and only your words clearly. Let your love and blessing be now upon father and mother. Help us all to continue to work together to make the earth more like heaven." I had three other questions, but only this one was addressed.

Then I heard these words. "You are asking more this morning than you have time or energy to hear, but lean back and let Me have unfettered control of your thoughts.

"First, know that I love you just as I do your father and mother and that death is the door through which you must go in order to fulfill my plan for your life. Your father is having the time of his life talking with so many old friends who have met him on the other side. They did not all come at once because they did not want to spoil the joy and wonder of his first views of the scenery in heaven.

"At first, he was met by his brother, Tom, and his mother, Nancy. Both looked as young as Bill remembered them when he was in his twenties. They took him into their arms in a warm hug and then Tom looked at Bill with a twinkle in his eye: 'Well, Sonny, you look as thin as a rail, like you haven't been eating properly. Just look at you!'

"At that moment Bill noticed his body. It was just like he had remembered it during his last weeks on earth, thin and emaciated. But as he looked, he saw an amazing transformation take place before his eyes. His body grew younger. The wrinkles began to fade away and he took on the appearance of a young man in his midthirties. The last thing to change was the bald spot on top of his head. When Tom asked him about this, Bill just smiled and said, 'I kind of like it this way.'

"Then Bill began to remember Thelma and the fact that she had been beside him during the last moments in his physical body. With this thought Bill found himself back in the little room in the nursing home. Thelma and a nurse were still there. Bill came up behind Thelma and put his arms around her and said, 'Darling, I love you. . . . I am safely out of this mess and you can dispose of this old body any way you want to. Don't cry too much. Don't feel sorry for yourself. I will be with you as you need me, but don't hold on to me. I am free at last. I know you cannot hear me now, but one day you will. Now I have to go. There are a lot of other folks that I want to see. Don't forget I still love you now more than ever.'[1]

"Instantly, Bill found himself back in the lovely garden he had seen a few moments before. A sparkling water fountain was surrounded by flowers of every color imaginable. Soon more friends began to come. For an unmeasured time, Bill was engrossed with the joy of renewed friendships.

"Once again, he felt drawn back to the earth and to his children. The moment he thought of them, he was with them and could see and hear what they were doing and saying. He looked in on Lincoln and Ruth just to give them his love. Then he thought of Laura Krarup [a friend in New Jersey] and found her with her mother. Bill saw Poul in the garden he [Poul] had helped to create. [Poul Krarup was a longtime friend who died a few months before Bill.]

"This is enough to give you a picture of what your father is doing. Some day you will have the joy of direct communication, but that is not yet."

---

1   In his final years, William Justice suffered from Alzheimer's disease. Lincoln Justice comments: "When one whose mind and ability to communicate were as strong as those of my father, it was especially sad to see him lose his ability to put together a full sentence as a result of Alzheimer's disease. My father was very clear that he did not want to have his physical body kept alive after it no longer served the needs of his spirit. He signed papers requesting that no life-support system be used to keep him alive. He wanted the doctors to stand back and let him die a natural death. When he saw that his body was failing and that he could no longer communicate, he refused to open his mouth to be fed or to drink water. His will was strong. Mercifully, the doctor honored the wishes of the family and suggested that the nurses not try to force him to eat or drink."

On September 8, the morning of the memorial service, or as we called it, "the graduation service," I heard these words as I prayed.

"You must be clear that the Communion of Saints that the Church believes in is actually a type of direct communication between the Church in heaven and the Church on earth. It is the direct link that God has created with all his people who have faith in his guidance.

"The forces of hell try every method to drive wedges of doubt and fear between God and his people in order to prevent this communication between heaven and earth. The voices of hell cast doubt by saying: 'All contact with the spirit world is of the devil, not God. How do you know that God is talking with you? How do you know that God has ever talked with people? Perhaps all the writers of the Bible were just suffering from hallucinations.'

"Satan wants to cut off communication between God and his people and to keep God's people on earth and those in heaven from communion with each other. See what he has done to people on earth. Christians in America are afraid to have open contact with their Christian brothers and sisters in Russia. Satan has divided Christian husbands and wives, children and parents.

"After my death and resurrection, the kingdom began to break upon the earth and spread with power through the whole earth. It seemed for a while that the kingdom of heaven was going to drive back the forces of darkness everywhere, but something happened that slowed the process. At the end of the third century, the Church was invaded by unconverted people who began to use the methods of hell. People began to use war and the weapons of fear and death in the name of the Prince of Peace. All over the world Christians began to fight other Christians. The kingdom of heaven retreated into monasteries and the true Church went underground. The dark ages of fear began.

"Now, today, more and more of the giant spirits have come to earth to prepare for another invasion of the earth with love. At the same time, the forces of hell and fear have taken into their hands the power of the atom and are prepared to destroy the physical earth in a mad attempt to keep the earth under their control.

"Your task and that of all God's people is to use only the weapons of the Spirit of God as you go into battle. The battle is not against people, but against the evil spiritual forces that would divide people from each other and from God.

"Take courage, for one more warrior has joined the forces in heaven. He will not give up on the earth but will continue to work with you to bring peace and love to earth."

Over the years I have shared in many of the experiences related in this book. It is with great joy that I can witness the fact that my faith in God and in the power of the Holy Spirit has grown stronger as a result of the fearless way that my father sought after truth. I have come to believe that now, as never before in history, the Spirit of Truth, the Holy Spirit, is guiding the human race into all truth (John 14 and 16:12–15). I believe there is nothing that is off limits for God's people to investigate.

This spirit of adventure has enriched my life and given me the courage to pioneer in many areas of life without fear. Jesus commanded his disciple to do two things: "Love God and each other" and "fear not!" It is the spirit of fear in its many forms that has paralyzed God's people and kept them from being used as God intends.

Outposts of the spirit are those outpoints along the front lines in which the brave pioneers of the human race have reached in their search for truth. My father was one of those pioneers. He has been on the front lines throughout his life.

Lincoln B. Justice

Afterword

A Brief Biographical Sketch of the Author

At 1:05 P.M. MST on August 31, 1985, William McKinley Justice, or Bill, as he was called by his friends, crossed over from this obstructed, physical plane of temporal life into the unobstructed universe of spiritual eternity.

Born October 2, 1903, near Killeen, Texas, the last of thirteen children of John Knox and Nancy Creighton Justice, Bill's earliest memories were of his home in a West Texas cotton patch. After graduation from high school in Belton, Texas, Bill earned a bachelor of arts degree cum laude from Southwestern University in Georgetown, Texas, in 1925.

On June 16, 1928, nearly three months before receiving his Master of Divinity degree from Southern Methodist University in Dallas, Bill married Thelma Minnie Dunagan—the best the Irish had to offer! More than a year and a half earlier, Bill had pointed out this attractive young librarian to a close friend, even before meeting her, and said something to the effect: "See that girl over there? I'm going to marry her some day." Bill had been watching Thelma and asking about this conscientious Sunday School teacher who had already developed a reputation for being a God-fearing Bible teacher.

During his forty-four-year ministry, Bill served fourteen pastoral appointments in the Methodist Church in Texas, New Mexico, New York, and New Jersey. After his first full-time appointment from 1928 to 1930 at Sanderson, Texas, Bill and Thelma came to Tularosa, New Mexico.

Bill's first public article was prophetic of his long career as a minister. On August 23, 1928, the *Dallas Morning News* headlined his article: "Says Preachers Must Speak on Moral Issues."

This type of attitude can get someone, even a preacher, into a peck of trouble. One way to handle a preacher like that, if the heat gets too uncomfortable for those in charge, is to see that he is appointed to small churches. But Pastor Justice could not be stopped that way, for his brilliant mind and flare for writing reached beyond the local papers to the most important organs read by the Christian community, scholars, and world leaders. These included: the *World Outlook*, the *Christian Advocate*, the *Methodist Quarterly*, the *Methodist Layman*, *Missionary Voice*, the *Christian Century*, the *Social Questions Bulletin*, and the *London Christian World*. He also wrote innumerable articles and letters published by the popular press, both in the United

States and Europe. Over the years, Bill's prolific pen produced more than fifty major articles and two books, *Our Visited Planet*, and *Safed the Sage: His Wit and Wisdom*, which he edited.

It was because he spoke out so strongly on moral issues and confronted immoral persons head-on that Bill eventually left the New Mexico Methodist Conference. He trod the steps he believed Jesus would have trod.

Bill was primarily responsible in 1933 for the unpopular stand on peace adopted at the Forty-Fourth New Mexico Annual Methodist Conference in session at Hot Springs (now known as Truth or Consequences):

"We furthermore declare that we will not, as a Christian Church, ever bless or sanction war." Bill not only believed that nations are under the same moral laws that apply to individuals, but he also relentlessly preached and wrote about peace.

For example, he wrote a well-researched treatise on why Americans should never have entered World War I. With the sweet taste of victory still in their mouths, who in America was going to buy that line of thinking? Patriotism, to most, meant a willingness to fight to the death for honor's sake when the nation called. Bill's way was to answer the call of Christ to love all people, even those our government has labeled "enemies."

Earlier than many Americans, Bill saw the war clouds gathering again. During the early and mid-1930s, when the leading industrialists and writers were warning the nation about the dangers of communism, Bill was busy with his pen warning about the growing menace of an unchristian group known as the National Socialist German Workers' Party under Adolph Hitler. It was only in the late 1930s that American industrialists, who had been discounting Hitler, began to take seriously the menace of Nazi Germany.

Bill could not bear arms any more than he could envision Jesus doing so. The more he spoke out against war, the more unpopular he became. It was the cross he chose. In this way, he discovered a strange inner peace that came from the awareness of the presence of Christ.

Bill's courageous confrontations of immorality in high places set him apart from other good men, even good preachers. His kind of courage in battle would have won anyone who could bear arms a medal of honor. His bloodless wounds as a pacifist and moralist were nevertheless deep and painful and could never have been borne by a coward.

There were two occasions in the early and late 1930s when Bill had the audacity to write articles about poorly paid Methodist ministers. He reminded Methodists that in the 1929–30 Book of Discipline there was in the "Social Creed of the Churches," a declaration supporting "a minimum wage in every industry." He proceeded to point out that 40 percent of Methodist preachers were paid less than a living wage while the other 60 percent received salaries ranging from adequate to on a par with other professions requiring advanced education.

Another issue that rankled many was his relentless objection to military chaplains being paid by the government and thereby subject to orders of military commanders. Ministers of God, Bill contended, should not take orders from the military. He pleaded for a system in some ways comparable to the Salvation Army and Red Cross that were serving the spiritual needs of soldiers independent of military commanders.

Bill's interest in an advanced degree led him to seek and obtain an appointment to churches near enough to Union Theological Seminary and Columbia University in New York City so that he could study there.

The South was restless and fitful in the 1960s, with repression of blacks and their civil rights. The Justice family was living in Stony Point, New York, in 1962 when Martin Luther King Jr. issued his invitation and challenge to ministers and laymen everywhere: "Come over to Macedonia and help us." Anyone familiar with Acts 16:6–10 knew that in August of that year, Macedonia was located at nearly every crossroad in the deep South.[1]

Bill joined seventy-four other ministers and laymen who could not resist this resounding call of Jesus through Paul and now Martin Luther King Jr. They set their faces like flint toward Albany, Georgia, as they rode in a caravan of cars. Bill thoroughly enjoyed riding with the Jewish rabbi who drove the car and relished the mission they set out to accomplish.

As these seventy-five ministers, priests, and rabbis began their prayer vigil on the Albany City Hall steps, they repeatedly ignored orders to disperse. One by one, they were arrested and put in makeshift jails, so many were they. A two-day fast reported in the newspapers all over the country succeeded in making Albany officials concerned and they let the seventy-five out on bail. I guess Bill was still out on bail when he entered glory.

This scholar and extraordinary teacher of the Bible was also noted for his great appreciation of classical literature and music, which he collected, read, and listened to. He was a noted authority who gave lectures to univer-

---

1   King's reference to Macedonia pertains to a vision sustained by Paul in which he was summoned by a man from Macedonia, the country lying immediately north of Greece. When Paul passsed from Asia to Europe on his second journey, of all the places in Europe, he first preached the gospel in Macedonia.

sity classes on the works of Dante, Browning, and Shakespeare. Bill was also a humorist. While at Tularosa, New Mexico, after one of Bill's sermons, Thelma, his wife, had confided that while his sermon was very good, his face showed only sternness and no humor. From that point forward, Bill cultivated the use of humor into a high art in his ministry and writing. Many friends recall having been invited to the Justice home for an evening of fun. At one of these gatherings my wife, Patsy and I were the youngest couple. I wondered how there could be so much fun at a retired Methodist minister's party. I soon found out. It was one of the most pleasant and memorable evenings I ever spent, with delightful humor mixed with rich wisdom. I laughed until I cried.

No great servant, man or woman, can give totally of himself or herself without a great spouse who makes possible the tremendous investment as a servant in public life. One of the finest jewels in Bill's life was Thelma, who made his ministry possible.

The one statement that best describes the life of Bill Justice is this:

He walked where Jesus would have him walk,
And he chose to be crucified with Him
As he lived for his Master.

William Yates
September 8, 1985
Las Cruces, New Mexico

Index

Hampton Roads Publishing Company

. . . for the evolving human spirit

Hampton Roads Publishing Company
publishes books on a variety of subjects including
metaphysics, health, complementary medicine,
visionary fiction, and other related topics.

For a copy of our latest catalog,
call toll-free, 800-766-8009,
or send your name and address to:

Hampton Roads Publishing Company, Inc.
1125 Stoney Ridge Road
Charlottesville, VA 22902
e-mail: hrpc@hrpub.com
www.hrpub.com